Tao Te Ching

A NEW TRANSLATION

Lao Tzu

TRANSLATED BY

William Scott Wilson

SHAMBHALA

Boston & London

2013

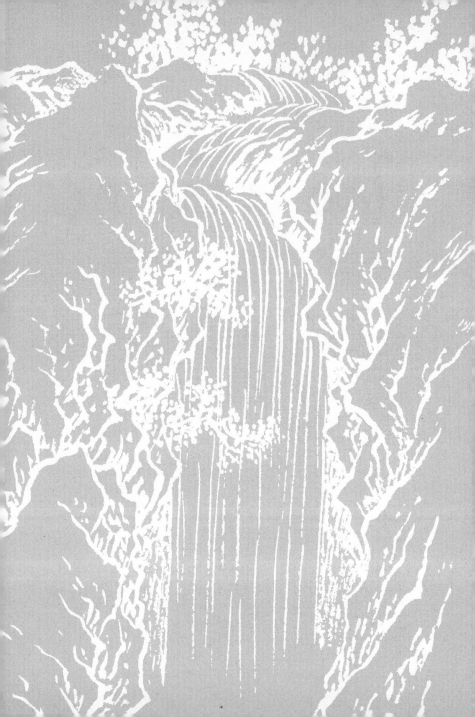

This translation is
dedicated to
Kathleen Marie Barnes

There is a road,
but it does not pass through this world.
—Han Shan

The beginning is the end.
—Heraclitus

Walking to where the waters end,
I sit and watch as the clouds rise.
—Wang Wei

The scenery of spring has no better or worse;
The flowering branches are,
of themselves, some long, some short.
—*P'u Teng Lu*

Emptiness laughs and nods in agreement.
—*Zenrin Kushu*

Shambhala Publications, Inc.
Horticultural Hall
300 Massachusetts Avenue
Boston, Massachusetts 02115
www.shambhala.com

English translation © 2010 by William Scott Wilson

The Great Seal Script sample on page x was brushed by artist
and calligrapher Shogo Kuroda.

9 8 7 6 5 4 3 2 1

First Paperback Edition
Printed in the United States of America

♾ This edition is printed on acid-free paper that meets the
American National Standards Institute Z39.48 Standard.
♻ This book is printed on 30% postconsumer recycled paper.
For more information please visit www.shambhala.com.

Distributed in the United States by Random House, Inc.,
and in Canada by Random House of Canada Ltd

The Library of Congress catalogues the previous edition of this
book as follows:

Laozi.
[Dao de jing. English]
Tao te ching: a new translation / Lao Tzu;
translated by William Scott Wilson.
pages   cm
Previously published: Tokyo: Kodansha International, 2010.
ISBN 978-1-59030-991-9 (hardcover)
ISBN 978-1-61180-077-7 (paperback)
I. Wilson, William Scott, 1944– , translator, writer of added
commentary. II. Title.
BL1900.L26E5 2012
299.5'1482—dc23
2011046438

CONTENTS

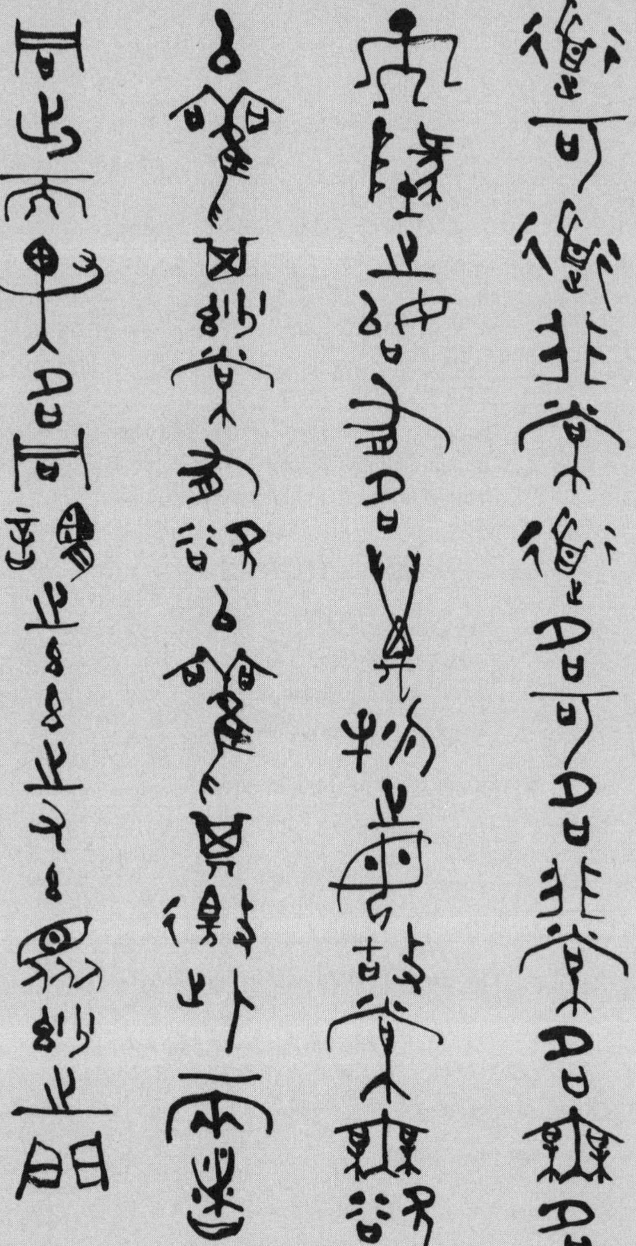

Returning to the Original Script of Lao Tzu's Times

The sample at the left illustrates the Great Seal Script, the style of writing used in China during the traditional dates given for Lao Tzu, and hence in the writing of the *Tao Te Ching* twenty-five centuries ago. The style has a beautifully patterned strength, and an astonishing wealth of nuance of meaning that far outstrips those found in the Chinese characters used today. Most of the characters of this script have survived because they were carved on early bronze, stone, and jade implements. Others were discovered on bamboo strips and silk.

It is not insignificant that this script was developed and in use at the time of the flowering of Chinese philosophy, known as the period of the Hundred Schools. Such men as Lao Tzu, Confucius, Mo Tzu, and the compilers and writers of the *Book of Songs*, the *I Ching*, and the *Spring and Autumn Annals* likely wrote and thought within the parameters of this script, and the mutual influence of artistic and philosophical insight between man and writing system cannot be ignored.

However, the Great Seal characters were abolished in 221 BCE by the great unifier of China, Ch'in Shih Huang Ti. As a result, versions of works originally written in the Great Seal Script were passed down in "rewritten" form, using a new set of characters. With this revision in the writing system, some of the nuance and meaning of the original characters was lost. The present translation goes back to the Great Seal system and reconstructs the text, coaxing out fresh nuance and meaning closer to the original intent of Lao Tzu.

PREFACE

I first encountered the old man during high school. A friend of mine and I frequently left campus during lunch in search of something more edible than school cafeteria fare, and, while out, would often drop in and browse at Little's Book Store, just a few blocks away from school. One afternoon, I asked the tall, elderly Mrs. Little (who would soon be arrested and briefly detained by undercover federal agents for selling them a copy of Henry Miller's *Tropic of Cancer*) for something interesting on Eastern religions or philosophy. She thought for a moment, went back to her office, and returned with a small paperback copy of the *Tao Te Ching*, translated by Paul Carus. I seem to recall that the cover of the book was a dark orange, made of thick non-glossy paper, and that it displayed a few mysterious Chinese characters. Looking inside, I found that each page of English had a corresponding opposite page of the Chinese text, and that it started right out with a disclaimer that stated, more or less, "If you think you have understood what's written here, you haven't understood it at all."

I felt that I had somehow received the keys to the kingdom.

I quickly purchased the little book, my friend bought a book on pottery, and off we went back to Silas Marner, geometry, and the impossible pronunciation of French.

Not long after that, my mother called me out to the dining room one night to look at something being aired on a new PBS station. The program was divided into two alternating segments. First, a blues guitarist by the name of Lightnin' Hopkins would play a song or two, and then the scene would switch to a young man in a crew cut who was lecturing on the book I had just purchased from Mrs. Little. The man talked with an intelligent and precise voice, and would every so often illustrate what he was discussing by writing Chinese characters on a blackboard. Then the program would return to the blues guitarist, and then once more back to the lecturer, a man by the name of Allen Watts.

I was dumbfounded. Nearly fifty years later, I still wonder if I have understood what PBS was getting at. Hopkins's riffs flowed like water, first like a torrent, next suddenly sustaining a note like a still pond, and then moving off in an entirely different direction. In the interim, Watts was explaining that the highest good was like water, which resides in the lowest places and yet benefits all creatures under heaven. Outside my house, the river we lived on moved quietly toward the Intercoastal Waterway and from there on to the Atlantic Ocean, reflecting every mood the day or season produced, never stopping or remaining the same even for a second. But it remained always the river, always the uninterrupted flow.

Most likely, the original text—if there was one—of a *Tao Te Ching* anywhere from 2,300 to 2,500 years old is not extant. Any number of copies exist, each with variations; some dating from relatively ancient times and some having been discovered as recently as 1993. Even among those texts, however, there seem to be none that can be dated earlier than the second century BCE. One of the most revered texts, the *Lao Tzu Tao Te Ching Chu*, was used by the Neo-Taoist scholar Wang Pi (226–49 CE), and it is this work that is often the basis of commentaries by Oriental scholars and for translations into foreign languages. This work was transmitted to Japan, possibly as early as the seventh century CE, and in 1770, Usami Shinsui (1710–76), a disciple of the philosopher Ogyu Sorai, published the highly respected *Ochu Roshi Dotokukyo* (*Wang's Commentary on Lao Tzu's Tao Te Ching*), considered to be a classic of scholarly research.

For the basis of the present translation and notes, I have relied heavily on the *Roshi-Soshi* (*Lao Tzu / Chuang Tzu*) by the scholars Fukunaga Mitsuji and Kozen Hiroshi, to whom I am greatly indebted. Their primary source was Shinsui's work, which in turn would place them in the lineage of Wang Pi.

It is often noted that the *Tao Te Ching* has been translated into more languages than any other book except the Bible,[1] and this without the zeal of evangelists seeking to substantiate their missions. As for translations into English, Wing-tsit Chan noted in 1963 that there were already about forty, and that number has probably more than doubled since then.[2]

There are a number of reasons for this. Foremost among these might be that the sheer beauty and transcendence of the language is a natural challenge to any translator. An integral part of that beauty and transcendence, however, is a meaning that is less than clear in many sections of the text; this, too, must tempt many people working with the language to try their hand at it.

Both of the above reasons—and of course the sublime philosophy of the work—apply to the present translator, but to them is added a third: the detective work involved in deciphering the

Chinese characters that may have been used originally, characters known as the Great Seal Script that have long since fallen out of the commonly used orthography, and that are now used only as a subset in the art of calligraphy. This will be further discussed in the introduction.

I would like to say that my copy of the Carus translation is still with me, but it eventually got lost in the shuffle of my peregrinations back and forth across the country, and eventually to Japan. The text, however, has always been within easy reach in one form or another ever since Mrs. Little sold me that first dark orange volume that so easily fit into one coat pocket after another. That first disclaimer, of course, has always haunted me, as it should haunt every reader, college professor, and translator. I have found, however, that the edge of that feeling may be somewhat smoothed by reading the book next to a moving body of water, a lake, or pond, or even while sitting in the tub.

In appreciation, I would like to thank the sainted Mrs. Little for first handing me this ever-changing key; my friend Gary Haskins, who was with me that day in Little's Book Store, and who has since worked with the Tao in shapes of clay; my mentor Ichikawa Tadashi, who for many years lectured me on the Way without my having been aware of it; my former editor Barry Lancet for providing me with the opportunity to work on one of the world's most remarkable pieces of literature; the many people who encouraged me in my translation work over the years: Kate Barnes, Jim Brems, John Siscoe, Jack Whisler, Tom Levidiotis, Justin Newman, Daniel Medvedov, and many others; my wife Emily for her constant

patience and understanding; and my late professors Hiraga Nobuo and Richard McKinnon, who kindly showed me that I was still adrift whenever I was sure that I had reached the other shore.

Any and all mistakes are my own.

William Scott Wilson

POSTSCRIPT: I have added a number of notes to the verses of the *Tao Te Ching* that I thought might clarify the text or be interesting to the reader. The quotes from the *Chuang Tzu* should be understood either as extensions of the philosophy of the work or as points of departure for further consideration.

INTRODUCTION

The Story

By the year 516 BCE, the old man had seen enough. Now eighty-eight years old, he had been Keeper of the Archives for the ancient Chou dynasty for some decades in the capital of Lo-yang, and over the years had watched the dynasty's steady decline. For centuries, principalities and feudal lords had constantly shifted alliances, titles had been arbitrarily bestowed on those who threw military power behind the aristocrats, stronger states within the empire had swallowed up the weaker ones, and internecine warfare had broken out in the capital.

Earlier the same year, a bright young and athletic scholar by the name of Chung-ni had come to visit the old man to ask how he might teach others the proper way of conducting the ancient rites, but the old man had answered that the men of old who had practiced such rites were now nothing but rotting bones, and that only their words remained. He added that "the good merchant keeps his wealth so deeply hidden that it seems he has nothing at all, and that even if a gentleman has great virtue, he maintains the appearance of a fool." The Keeper of the Archives then ended the interview by

advising the young man to "abandon his haughty attitude, many desires, flamboyant posture, and self-indulgent ambition." Chung-ni concluded that he had just encountered a dragon.

Not long after this, the old man, who had always favored simplicity, packed what belongings he had into an oxcart and headed west. At the Han-ku Pass, which marked the last frontier of Chou rule, he was recognized by the warden of the pass, and, before being given permission to continue through, was to write down something of what he had learned as Keeper of the Archives. This the old man did in a short work of some five thousand archaic Chinese characters. Then, without further ado, he "lit out for the territories."

The Background

The Chou dynasty (1122–255 BCE),[1] which the old man had served, was established when King Wu invaded the old capital and captured and killed Chou Hsin,[2] the last king of the preceding Shang dynasty (1766–1122 BCE). The Chou had originally been an agricultural people living to the west of the center of Shang political and military power. As the Chou grew in strength and influence, and as the situation in the empire deteriorated, the Shang finally took the Chou leader, King Wen,[3] hostage, presumably for their own security. This, alas, precipitated the war that would be their undoing.

The Chou were not a large clan, but ruled, apparently, by both charismatic dignity and delegation. After defeating the Shang, the Chou assigned fiefs and principalities to a large number of relatives, sub-chiefs, and unrelated allies, and even to those Shang descendents who could not be conquered but who would now pledge their allegiance to the Chou. These feudal assignments tended to develop into city-states—possibly numbering about one thousand at the beginning of the dynasty—and each vassal was given a clearly ranked

title in a binding hierarchy. The Chou ruled from the center, constantly balancing its alliances and refereeing the territorial disputes that arose among the various dukes, marquises, counts, and barons.

The concept of rule in Chou times requires some clarification. The modern Chinese character for "king," 王, was the designation of the highest ruler and seems to have been derived from a number of different ancient characters: one meaning a propped-up ax, in which case the meaning is clear; and another simply meaning big, and by extension, powerful. But yet another ancient character is in approximately the same form as the modern one, and shows a vertical line connecting the three horizontal lines designating Heaven, Earth, and Man;[4] and indeed, the Shang concept of rule, inherited by the Chou, was most likely a form of politico-religious shamanism in which the king, or chief shaman, mediated between the people and whatever gods they worshipped or propitiated. Later, he would become the man who conducted the most important rites to insure the harmony between Heaven, Earth, and Man.

This became the absolute practice with the ascendancy of the Chou, who not only respected the ancient rites of the Shang and were determined to continue them, but who also believed from their own experiences as agriculturists that the activities and conduct of Heaven, Earth, and Man were mutually influenced. Thus, if the ceremonies and rites were not conducted correctly, the world would be out of order.

The Chou people were not unsophisticated. But comparing themselves with the highly cultured Shang, they felt the need for professional assistance. In this way, the propriety-minded Chou rulers found it necessary to engage the old Shang priests to perform and eventually transmit the proper way of performing rites and to teach the ethics and morality that insured them. These teachers and performers formed a new class in Chou society, and would eventually be designated as "scholars." Both the old man and the enthusiastic scholar Chung-ni belonged to this group.

By the time Chung-ni had his disconcerting encounter with the old man in 516 BCE, the Chou dynasty had lost a great measure of its political and military power, and its kings were mostly relegated to certain religious and ceremonial roles. In 771 BCE, some two hundred and fifty years before, an alliance of feudal states from the north attacked the Chou capital and killed its king before being repulsed by another group. The new ruler, a Chou prince, moved east to the capital of Lo-yang, and from this time became ruler in title only. And even his title was not sacrosanct. In 704 BCE, the feudal lord of Wu had himself proclaimed king, or *wang*, of that state, thus subverting the Chou ruler's religious authority. In the south, the state of Ch'u began dominating a huge area along the Yang-tze River, and called its ruler the *wang* from the very beginning, further deteriorating the Chou king's prestige.

During this time, the feudal lords chose to either forget or ignore their ancient blood ties and alliances with the Chou, and made outright grabs for power, taking new territories and new titles; large states devoured the small, barons became dukes, and generals became marquises. Of the ancient city-states, barely two hundred remained; among those, only ten stood out as viable and likely to survive.

By the sixth century BCE, the temporal and religious authority of the Chou was in eclipse, and many of the time-honored traditions were being abandoned or changed to fit the needs of the new rulers. The military (*wu*, 武) had clearly outstripped the cultural (*wen*, 文), and the ensuing imbalance was clear to at least one group of men: the scholars.

From the very beginning, the duty of the scholars was to recall the old traditional rites and ceremonies, and, as society deteriorated, they advocated the conscientious return of values such as human-heartedness (仁), loyalty (忠), righteousness (義), and even the proper names and titles of the aristocratic hierarchy that were now being bought, traded, or simply taken by force. Chung-ni, who would later be given the title of Master Kung-fu (known to us as Confucius), laid special emphasis on this last problem, declaring that words and titles should be made clear, for once terms were cheapened or not used as they ought to be, public discourse becomes confused, and thinking becomes muddled. He called this correct usage of terms the "rectification of names" (正名). By his time there were a number of works considered by the scholars to be "classics," and it was to these histories, records, and collections of poetry that these men could refer and quote in order to guide whichever ruler they might be advising back to ways that would promote peace and harmony.[5]

As Keeper of the Archives, the old man would have had access to a great number if not all of these documents, and so would have been the best source for the ambitious young reformer Chung-ni to consult. Thus the latter's astonishment at the old man's response, and his bewilderment at who (or what) the old man really was.

The Old Man and His Book

We know next to nothing about the Keeper of the Archives. Some four hundred years after his death, the Grand Historian Ssu-ma Ch'ien (145–86? BCE) wrote the bare bones of the above story, including some other details that appear very much like folk myth, and which add nothing to our understanding of the man. Ssu-ma Ch'ien does note that the old man's family name was Li, his personal name Erh, and his posthumous name Tan. This, too, tells us little, as Li (李), meaning a kind of plum, is a common family name; and both Erh (耳) and Tan (耽) indicate "ear" (or "pendulant ear" in the case of Tan), signifying listening, and by extension, wisdom. It is perhaps interesting that the plum indicated is described as blossoming in the spring with white flowers, the same color that whatever hair was left on the old man would have been after eighty-eight years; and that its taste is said to be both sweet and tart, much as his words may be perceived. In those times, this same character also meant to "suppress" or "govern"; and a *li hsing* (李行) was a messenger. All of this, however, adds only a mythic quality to the old man's name, and gives off the faint scent of apocrypha.

Today, the old man is known to us as Lao Tzu (老子), literally "old child," and this, too, presents a problem. *Tzu* can be a suffix which is often attached to the names of certain Chinese philosophers[6] and has taken on the meaning of "Master." The ancient character for *lao* depicted a man with long hair and a bent back carrying a staff, and indicated such a man, usually over seventy, often with virtue to match his years. Thus, the name Lao Tzu could be taken as simply "The Old Master" or more colloquially, "Master Old Guy." Or, for reasons to be discussed later, "The Old Masters." Complicating the problem is that *lao* also designated an official (Chan suggests "viscount")[7] or an official who has retired. As a final twist, scholars now argue whether the author of this book was the old man in question or another old man with the same name.

Ssu-ma Ch'ien mentions that the Keeper of the Archives was a native of the southern state of Ch'u, and this does add an interesting clue about the old man, not so much as to his identity, but rather to his spiritual and psychological disposition. Ch'u was at a relatively far remove from the Chou capital and culture, and, although "Chinese," had its own unique traditions. The poetry of its famous *Ch'u Tzu*, or *Songs of Ch'u*, dated from about the seventh century BCE, is darker and more brooding than the poetry of the north, is full of erotic imagery and reference to fragrant plants, and contains a series of songs that may have been formulaic chants for shamanistic rites. Indeed, the state of Ch'u is deeply associated with shamanism, a practice that by the sixth century was held in approbation by Chung-ni and his fellow scholars,[8] who apparently held shamans to be of the same ilk as musicians, jugglers, and actors.

Further, the translator Red Pine informs us that the Ch'u rulers took for their surname the word *hsiung*, or "bear,"[9] the worship of which goes back to the Paleolithic, and so may have promulgated, or at least reflected, this element in the Ch'u culture. Shamans in parts of Asia are described as wearing bearskins, and it is said that the mythic culture hero Yu wore bearskins, stepped like a bear, and in some ways personified the bear spirit. Interestingly, the original Chinese character for bear, 熊, meant something like "shining brightly like the light of a fire."

The nexus between Ch'u bearskins and the old man's book is this: shamanism tends to emphasize the unknown, the intuitive, and the left-handed approach to knowledge, and regards the rational thinking of Chung-ni and his scholars as so much empty play on the surface of the world; much of this can be found in between the lines of the manuscript the old man left with the warden of the pass. Or, more blatantly if enigmatically stated in the lines themselves:

> For this reason, the sage
>> Covers himself with rough clothes of animal fur, and
>>> holds the stringed jewels close to his chest.   VERSE 70

Finally, this interesting note:

> He who, forgetting the limitations and false measurements of humanity, could rightly imitate the behavior of animals—their gait, breathing, cries and so on—found a new dimension of life: spontaneity, freedom, "sympathy" with all the cosmic rhythms, and, hence, bliss and immortality.[10]

When the warden of the pass asked the old man to write down a summary of what he had learned while Keeper of the Archives, it would seem that the old man did not want to waste much time at the task. What he left behind was a short work of about 5,250 characters, almost no structure, no punctuation whatsoever, and no title. The style, while not exactly haphazard, is varied: over twenty differing forms of verse interspersed with prose or prose-poetry. Themes may show some constancy for a verse or two, but then may change radically into what seem like complete non sequiturs. All in all, the reader is left with the impression that either the old man was giving the warden of the pass a tour de force of style, or that he was in many cases quoting maxims and aphorisms from the past.

If the latter is so, then the old man was perhaps less the writer of the work than a compiler and editor of wisdom he had gleaned from the Chou Archives over so many years. Hence the eventual first title, *Lao Tzu*, or *The Old Master*, may have meant in a language with no clear plurals, *The Old Masters*.[11] Some four hundred years later, the book was divided into eighty-one chapters or distinct verses,[12] and it was about that time that the historian Ssu-ma Ch'ien perhaps coined the word "Taoist School" in his great work the *Shih*

Chi. Ssu-ma Ch'ien also noted that the book concerned the Tao and virtue,[13] and it is apparently from this time that the book was called the *Tao Te Ching*, or *The Classic of the Way and Its Virtue*.

As to the language of the book, it must be noted that Chinese, as a language based on ideographs, reached crises from time to time when the growth of concepts and ideas outstripped the modes of expression. The sixth century BCE seems to have been one of those periods, and the language of the old man's book sometimes expresses such an inadequacy. It is at times astonishingly vague, at times layered with meanings, although this in itself may indicate another factor: that its verses were being pulled from languages even older than the old man's. Or even languages quite different.

In ancient times, the area we call "China" today was divided into as many as eight different cultural groups and, although they gradually became what might be called "Chinese," the languages and written characters were not unified[14] until some three hundred years after the *Tao Te Ching*, or *Lao Tzu*, was written. This poses an interesting problem for the translator of the work, as he or she may then wonder what the language was, and what the characters were that appeared from beneath the old man's brush.

The Translation

By the time the old man was finishing up work at the archives, there were a number of differing forms of written characters in use, many of which would have been familiar to him. These varying styles had developed throughout the Chou dynasty in the individual states, and been used not only by scholars, but no doubt by the aristocracy, merchants, and craftsmen as well. Generally included under the broad term Great Seal Script (*Ta Chuan*), they have been left to us on bronze, stone, and jade, as well as on bamboo slips and silk. And although the structures of the characters are similar to those used by modern Chinese[15]—either pictorial in nature or a meaning radical combined with a character or part of a character indicating its sound[16]—visually they are quite different, and offer a much broader range of nuance and playfulness than the standardized and simplified current forms.

Thus, the modern character for "fear" or "respect" is written 畏, which gives no hint of a fuller meaning during the old man's time. The Great Seal character, however, depicts a demon brandishing a rod or stick, and thus provides a more vivid connotation to the term. Other examples might include the character 燕, which in the old man's days meant to "enjoy" or "relax" and in the Great Seal character depicts a swallow—its current meaning—in soaring flight; the word "few," 寡 in modern Chinese, but in the old character showing us summer under a roof—how many people would stay indoors on a summer day?; to "pardon" 免, which again indicates nothing visually in the modern character, but which in the Great Seal style illustrates a woman giving birth to a child, and thus adds the nuance of being pardoned and given a new life; or the word to "bring up" or "raise" (a child) 育, which in the ancient script clearly depicts a child being delivered from its mother's womb.

The old man—the highly educated Keeper of the Archives—wrote his book in some form of the Great Seal characters; and one of the guiding principles of this current work has been to base the translation on those ancient ideographs and their etymologies in order to be as true to the original meaning as possible. In a number of cases, the comparison of the modern script and the ancient yielded no significant difference, while in others, a meaningful expansion of nuance was astonishingly evident. Similarly, there were times when those nuances could be readily—if not artistically—expressed, while in others, there was almost no way to add

them to the text. The question has been how the text would have been written by the old man, and how it might have appeared to those contemporaries who would have read it.

Some three hundred years after the old man lit out for the territories, Ch'in Shih Huang Ti destroyed the remaining states under the Chou dynasty and established his new empire. A practical man, he was impressed neither by the squabbling schools of scholars that had proliferated under the Chou, nor by the many books they had written that might cause dissention and unrest among his subjects. Therefore, to the extent possible, he exterminated the former and burned the latter. No doubt a number of scholars prudently turned to agriculture or other pursuits before the calamity reached them, and buried their books, hoping to dig them up again when the time was ripe.[17] The original book passed on to the warden of the pass was one of the works that did not survive, or at least was buried deep in a place yet undiscovered. In returning to the ancient script, however, and comparing it with that of the texts that remain, we may get a fuller idea of what the old man had in mind and how he was inclined to pass it on.

The Interior

The old man's book is, in large part, about not doing things. This is not *not* doing things at all, but doing them by not doing them to their detriment. In the same way, it is about letting things go and allowing them to get themselves done. This is following a completely Unchartered Path and, as the old man's later disciple Chuang Tzu said, taking up "free and easy wandering." The old man called this a mystery. His descendents, the Zen monks, called it a stone woman giving birth to a child at midnight.

What does that mean?

During the old man's time, there was any number of talented men advising people—not only kings and aristocrats, but nearly anyone who would listen—how to live through the difficult times they struggled with. Chung-ni and generations of scholars studied the old classics for guidelines, and taught that applying the past to the present was, indeed, the Way.[18] When he and other scholars advocated "Renew yourself just a little every day, and then day by day, and then yet again,"[19] he was talking about both the rites and ceremonies of the past, and the proper mental attitude with which they had been conducted. Chung-ni also developed the concept that those who listened to him and did things in this way would truly be *Chun-tze* (君子), a term that meant "prince" in high antiquity, but that now was to mean "Gentleman." Thus, the Way had already been established and was there to follow. This, however, would require great effort. Or in other words, some doing.

The old man rejected all this.

We have already read his comments on the "men of old"—King Wen, King Wu, and the Duke of Chou[20]—that they were nothing but rotting bones, and that only their words remained. Chung-ni and the scholars that came before him, of course, revered those words, stood by them, and did their best to transmit them to a declining age. He commented often on his reverence for words themselves, and along with his advocacy of the Rectification of Names—making sure that words were used correctly—he added that "When it comes to a Gentleman's language, he takes nothing lightly."[21]

In the first and perhaps polestar verse of the old man's book, he turns this scholastic love of words on its head with this phrase:

道可道、非常道

The Way that can be articulately described
　　is not the Unchanging Way. VERSE I

This is a terse, multilayered pun that requires further discussion, but even at face value, it might be paraphrased as "All of your intelligent talk will not lead you to the Way." And in case the point is missed, he immediately follows this line with

名可名、非常名

> The name that can be said out loud
>   is not the Unchanging Name.   VERSE 1

This is certainly a direct challenge to the scholars' emphasis on the Rectification of Names; it states that words and verbally built concepts are off-base, and implies that they may indeed lead us astray. Again, this is the foundation of the old man's book, and the bedrock upon which his own five thousand words are to be understood.[22]

Chung-ni and the scholars, however, were not concerned with words alone. The Gentleman was one who could and *would* put things to right; he was one who studied assiduously and did his best to have that study applied to the world. A phrase that would stir them to action time and time again and keep them from sloth is found in the *I Ching*, an ancient book venerated by both the Confucian and Taoist schools:

君子終日乾乾

> The Gentleman is unceasingly and energetically active throughout the entire day.

This advocacy of energetic action and wakefulness was further emphasized in a famous section of the *Analects*, the collection of sayings, deeds, and thoughts of Chung-ni and his disciples:

Tsai Yu was sleeping during the day. The Master [Chung-ni] said,

"You cannot carve a rotten piece of wood; you cannot trowel a wall made of dung. To what purpose would you criticize Yu?"

In contrast, the old man painted a very different picture of how men practiced the Way in the past:

> Hesitating, like crossing a stream in winter;
> Wavering, like fearing demons with clubs on all sides;
> Respectful, like being a guest;
> Pliant, like ice about to melt ... VERSE 15

To the old man, the man of the Way did not rush to the fore with advice, but remained in low places and out of sight, until coming out could not be avoided. Even then, however, he was to seem "dim as dusk, while the average man sees everything in detail" (verse 20). "Auspicious traveling [being in the world]," he notes, "leaves neither ruts nor tracks" (verse 27). As for changing the world, the old man declares

> The world is an instrument regulated by the gods,
> And cannot be fabricated into something else.
> He who tries to do this will damage it.
> He who tries to grasp it will lose it. VERSE 29

In the end, the sage does not fabricate, meddle, or try to redirect the world. On the contrary, his role is more in helping things along. Thus he concludes that the sage "Does not fabricate, but things come to fruition" (verse 47); that "tranquility defeats the heat [rather than energetic reform]" (verse 45); that "if you know when to stop [and maybe take a nap like Tsai Yu], you will not stand on shaky ground" (verse 44). The Way, according to the old man, "never acts, yet no act is left undone" (verse 37).

Thus, the old man and Chung-ni had very different visions of what the Way and acting in the world might be. For Chung-ni, the Way was chartered, and action—whether in study or politics—was a lively moving forward. For the old man, any chartered Way was wrong from the start. As for Chung-ni's vigorous and positive action, the old man would have none of it. And, although there is some matter of definition here, he would often have us not act at all.

Key Terms of the Tao

The old man wrote his book about 2,500 years ago in an archaic script that often bears little resemblance to the Chinese characters used today. Therefore, it is necessary for the translator to work through the etymology of each character for both its ancient meanings and its broader nuances; and while it is beyond the scope of this translation to provide an accompanying etymological dictionary to the old man's text, it may be helpful to provide the reader with a short explanation of a few key terms. As is often the case in working with Oriental languages, however, there are some terms and concepts that do not easily lend themselves to an Occidental equivalent. The very first word of both the title and text of the old man's book—the term that is the pivot of all his remarks—is a case in point.

Tao

This term, "Tao" (道), has been the nemesis of translators ever since early times. One of the first to ask about its meaning was a prince from eastern India who, wishing to read the book, requested a number of translators to explain it to him. The translators were Buddhists and did their best with the Sanskrit terms available. One of them linked *Tao* to the term *marga*, meaning a track, path, or

way by which one arrives at enlightenment. To him, it was clear that the path is the cause that leads us to the result, the enlightened mind (Sanskrit: *bodhi*). The other translation team declared that just the opposite was true. They interpreted *Tao* as *bodhi*: knowledge, understanding, or pure wisdom. In this way, the Tao does not cause or lead to enlightenment, it is enlightenment itself. The prince was left to draw his own conclusions.

In Western languages, the first Latin translator (name unknown) interpreted the word as *ratio*, derived from the word for "reason." Later, more sophisticated terms like *natura naturans*—nature naturing—were employed to indicate that the Tao was an ongoing process, not one complete as in the sense of *natura naturata*. Similar to the Latin *ratio*, the Greek term used was *logos*, again from "reason" or "speak," as in being logical. In English, words as dissimilar as "nature," the "highest good," or the "Path" or "Way" are common attempts to convey a sense of the word. A number of translators simply give up, and use the word "Tao," hoping that the Chinese itself will become clear by context. This is not a bad choice.

According to the Chinese dictionaries, there seem to have been a number of Great Seal characters for "Tao," but all contain a radical element for "movement" or "stepping along," and the radical for "head." The latter has been explained as a phonetic element, but in many cases, the phonetic elements for a Chinese character include some sense of its meaning. In the character "Tao," the head radical is dominated by the character for "eye," denoting observation or passive intelligence; while the motion radical on top indicates continual movement. Thus, along with the basic meaning of "road," "path," or anciently "to lead," "Tao" can also mean a moving intelligence, without a created beginning or end, and by implication "self-generated." It is often equated with *tzu jan* (自然), the "spontaneous" or the "Of-Itself-So."

The old man often used "Tao" as a part of the term "The Way of heaven" (天之道). By his time, the word "heaven" (天) no longer indicated an anthropomorphic deity as it had during the Shang dynasty, but rather the impersonal workings of the universe. Its Way was understood as an intelligence or principle pervading the cosmos which, if harmonized with, would result in a complete human being. Thus, the old man could not have disagreed more with Chung-ni and his scholars, who declared that "It is Man that is able to make the Way great, not the Way that makes Man great."[23] On the contrary, for the old man,

> The Way is the storehouse and kitchen of
>   the Ten Thousand Things.
> It is a treasure for the good man who is a blessing to all,
> And a place of support for the bad man, as it would carry
>   him on its back as though he were a child.   VERSE 62

Chung-ni looked first to humanity; the old man looked first to the Tao.

In the larger sense, Tao is the Way of Life: it is both imminent and transcendent; it

> . . . drifts buoyantly, now left, now right. . . .
> The Ten Thousand Things rely on it,
>   and are born without fanfare. . . .
> It clothes and nourishes the Ten Thousand Things,
>   but does not assume to be their master.   VERSE 34

Learn to practice this imminent Tao, and you will be on your way to "free and easy wandering." Approaching this from a slightly different tack, Lieh Tzu notes the following, putting Chung-ni in the role of a Taoist.

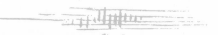

Yan Hui asked Chung-ni, "Some time ago, I crossed the deep pool at Shang-shen. The ferryman handled the boat like a god. I asked, 'Can you study to handle a boat like this?' 'Indeed, you can,' he said. 'Anyone able to swim can learn, and a good swimmer will get the knack of it easily. Now, as for a diver, he could get up and handle a boat though he had never seen one before.' I continued to question him, but he would inform me of nothing else. May I be so bold as to ask what you think of this?"

Chung-ni said, "Well now, I've been amusing myself with you with shapes and patterns for a long time, but have not yet come to the real pith of things. Have you indeed grounded yourself in the Way? Anyone who swims may learn because he takes the water lightly. A good swimmer can get the knack of it because he doesn't think about the water at all. Now as for a diver, he handles a boat without ever having seen one before; he sees a deep pool as though it were dry land, and a swamped boat as though it were just an overturned cart. The Ten Thousand Things may be swamped and overturned and lined up in front of him, but they will be unable to disturb his tranquility. Will he not be at peace wherever he goes?"[24]

In a narrower sense, the word "Tao" has come to mean a "practice," something one follows and studies, and makes into *a* way of life. This is the sense we understand especially when speaking of the Way of Tea, the Way of Calligraphy, the Way of the Brush, or even the Way of Karate. But whether you follow the larger Way or a more particular way—which may lead or provide hints to the larger—there is something transformative you begin to realize in the process.

Te

The Grand Historian Ssu-ma Ch'ien had mentioned that the old man's book was concerned with Tao and *te*, and around the first century BCE, it began to be known as the *Tao Te Ching*—the *Classic of Tao and Te*—with several attempts being made to divide and number the verses in various combinations. About this time, a Ho-shang Kung divided the book into eight-one verses, the first thirty-seven of which are set as the chapter on Tao, and those following organized as the chapter on *te*. It can be assumed, then, that these two terms are the twin focal points of the work. Indeed, the two concepts fit together very much like yin and yang and, once separated, lose much of their deeper meaning.

The term "*te*" (德) is variously defined as "power" or "virtue," not in the Confucian moral sense, but as in the old English of *vertu*—the intrinsic excellence or focus of any object, animate or inanimate.[25] It is the natural potency of every phenomenon. But as the sources of the old man's book appear to be multiple, so are the nuances of this word "virtue," and the reader must be careful to note the context within which it appears. Generally speaking, however, the old man valued virtue that was unfabricated. That is, virtue without pretense or self-consciousness.

Anciently, 德 appears to have been written with the character "direct" (直) over the character "heart/mind" (心), with the extended meaning of "straight," "upright," or "honest." Eventually, this old character was abandoned for the one currently in use, and meant, in the old man's time, something like the strength or ability to understand the gods or the mysterious. Interestingly, it could be substituted with the character *te* (得), indicating a hand picking up a shell (an ancient currency) along the road, and later, simply to "obtain." Both characters included the meaning of obtaining something that would nourish the heart or mind. In the *I Ching*, with which the old man would have been quite familiar, we find:

君子進德修業

The Gentleman advances in *te*,
And cultivates his knowledge.

Not only the Gentleman, but every creature, every rock, and every blade of grass possesses or is filled with its own *te*. *Te* is its true natural character. It is what remains after the baggage has been thrown overboard.

If the Tao might be thought of as the ever-flowing intelligent movement of a field of events, *Te* may be considered to be the particular foci or individual events in that field. On a personal human basis, this event is one's true innate nature—etymologically speaking, the heart/mind with which one is born—and in cultivating and being true to this unique character, he cultivates his own *te*. Doing this, he integrates the event of his own life with the Tao itself. Or in other words, he has integrity. In the *Chung Yung*, a book with sources predating the old man and Chung-ni, this is expressed in this way:

天命之謂性、卒性之謂道、修道之謂教

Heaven's command is called one's innate character. Following one's innate character is called the Way. Cultivating the Way is called education.

Thus, the Tao/*te* relationship is not separable—one cannot be isolated from the other. As Chuang Tzu put it:

What I call good is not human-heartedness or righteousness. Good lies within your own *te*. What I call good is not human-

heartedness or righteousness. It means shouldering the purport of the innate nature (性) mandated you.

The individual, however, is not the only point of focus on the grid of the Tao, and the True Person—the Taoist version of the Confucian Gentleman—must take into account the *te* of all other points of focus he or she may encounter. If this can be done, the borderline between self and other begins to dissolve, and each aspect of individuation can be understood as one aspect or component of the Tao. In social life, this means understanding and behaving appropriately to the *te* of all those you encounter, thus creating a seamless harmony of individuals. In the arts, this may be understood by the woodcutter or potter following his own natural *te* and that of his medium as well. For the swimmer, the same link is necessary for natural and efficacious swimming in either flat pools or rapids. For the butcher, it applies to the art with which he cuts up the ox. Both the individual and the medium are transformed in their interaction, and yet both retain their true natures.

How can this be done?

Wei—Fabrication

The old man recommended that we do things without doing them. That we act without acting.

The character *wei* (為) usually means to "do" or "act," but this is not a complete understanding of the term. There were several differing versions of this character in the old Great Seal characters, some of them illustrating an animal or a hand next to an animal, and denoting shape or man-made shape, and thus "provisional" or "imitation." Over time, an imitated or mimicked form led to the definition of "make" or "do," but as one might fabricate something.

Wei, then, is related to the homonym *wei* (偽), "to falsify or deceive," as the latter is the same character with the radical for "man" at its left. Thus, to do or act is never far from fabrication or acting in the theatrical sense of the word. It has a tendency to be not quite "real."

According to the old man, in order to act "for real," there must be nothing extra between the mind, the body, and the action itself. We cannot be laden with intention or mental baggage; we must act naturally[26] and without coercion. His phrase *wei wu wei* (為無為), "to act without acting" or "to do without doing," means to act without assertiveness, without relying on human mental constructs or notions or rules. It is to act spontaneously according to one's innate nature, and in harmony with the innate natures of all things in the environment. For him, to act without acting, to do without fabrication is to be in harmony with the Tao. In his book, he says repeatedly that the sage

為而不恃

"... Acts, but relies on nothing"   (translated variously
according to context in VERSES 2, 10, 51, 77)

and this is closely related to his remark that

聖人之道為而不争

The Way of the sage is to act but not contend   (VERSE 81)

with either circumstances, the environment in total, or the people with whom we come into contact. To do this we must return to the ancient character for *te*—the character with the radical for "direct" over the radical for "heart/mind"—and engage the world with a direct, intuitive, and spontaneous understanding from which any action cannot be divorced.

In this way, an understanding of the word *wei*—to act, make, or fabricate—and the phrase *wei wu wei*—to act without fabrication—is pivotal to a true grasp of the old man's book. Without ridding action of the ego or mindful intent, neither the expression of one's own true nature or talent (*te*) nor true appreciation—appreciation without the intervention of self-interest—of the "other" is possible. And without the free play of *te*, or the points of focus on the field, the Tao cannot flow with the spontaneity that defines it. It is only this activity—or rather the nonactivity of *wu wei*—that can integrate the individual's *te* with the entire field of the Tao, and it is only this integration that will allow the full development and maturity of one's individual character.

Again, Chuang Tzu offered a slightly different approach:

Civilian and military affairs each have their capabilities, but the Great Man has no self-interest in either. For this reason, their [or his] *te* is assured. Each of the Ten Thousand Things has its own principle, but the Tao is not partial to any. Thus, they are without name. Being without name, they do not act. They do not act, but nothing is left undone.

When you deal with names, when you act according to forms, by the time you have grasped them the field has changed and you will be left with only definitions and illusions. The "real world" and your true potential will have passed you by.[27]

The Perennial Philosophy

> *Things are complex, but one does not worry about their being chaotic; they change, but one does not worry about their being confused.* —Wang Pi[28]

The people of China and the Far East have had a long time—about twenty-five centuries—to think about the old man's little book. And they have been happy to do so. It has been de rigueur reading for every educated and cultured man in China since ancient times, and, it has been noted, more commentaries have been written on it than any other Chinese classic.[29] Moreover, the ideas that have been extracted from this work—along with his disciples' subsequent works, the *Chuang Tzu* and the *Lieh Tzu*—have formed a great part of what might be termed the Oriental Perennial Philosophy. A very bare-bones summary of this philosophy might be as follows:

The world, and indeed the universe, is not something created by a deity, but is rather a self-generating spontaneous process embraced by a nature that is immanent in all things. This being so, there is nothing that is separate or beyond the universe, or outside of the constantly changing continuum in which we all exist. The most basic stuff that underlies all things is *ch'i*, a vital force or psycho-physical material energy that is neither completely spirit nor matter. *Ch'i*'s modalities begin with a division into yin and yang, further develop into the basic elements of earth, water, fire, metal, and ether, and from there transform into the Ten Thousand Things. This last term encompasses everything from heaven and spirits, to mountains, rivers, the wind, rain, and all creatures including ourselves; *ch'i* being transformed into one and then another. This chain of being, this Great Transformation, is both interconnected and interdependent, forming the flowing grid or field of existence that is our natural home. Thus, we are "at home" in the universe every bit as much as all other natural phenomena, with which we share the modalities of this basic *ch'i*. We are part and parcel of the Great Transformation that is the ever-changing world.

To act in accord with this spontaneously changing continuum, it is necessary to act as though we were integrated with it, and not as something apart, which we are not. This has become a problem for most of us for a number of reasons, two of which are paramount.

The first is our tendency toward greed and desire that coagulates or calcifies what should be a placeless place on the grid. This causes a condition of stagnation, leading to a sense of being apart from the world, rather than a part of it. Freedom from selfishness and grasping (or holding on) means the freedom to once again fully enjoy our participation in the Great Flow of things. The Way, this philosophy contends, is in knowing when you have enough; encumbered (with either material or intellectual goods), you will not move freely. The old man notes that "if you desire something excessively, you will invariably have great expenses" (verse 44). In this sense, the price of moving freely is far less than that of the baggage we load upon ourselves.

Our second greatest stumbling block is our constant need to conceptualize, judge, and attach value to things, thereby falsifying our experience in the world.[30] "Exterior" to ourselves, this conceptualization places our own created ideas between us and the natural world; "interior" to ourselves, we cannot even grasp our very own nature. On our own, we place a filter not only between our experience and ourselves, but between our fundamental nature and ourselves. To rectify this problem, we are encouraged to "act without acting," and to leave our forms, names, and fabrications behind.[31]

Chuang Tzu relates that when perceiving the world, we must perceive it with our *ch'i* rather than our external organs[32] or even our mind, and thus be open to the patterns and reverberations not only of the natural world, but of our own. The old man equated the fulfillment of nonfabrication with the perception of wordless teachings, and noted how few in the world can grasp such things.

The Perennial Philosophy urges us to listen to nature and to ourselves, for they amount to the same thing. We are to proceed with spontaneity, to throw our mental baggage overboard, and to live our lives in an excursion of "free and easy wandering" along with all the other Ten Thousand Things. With an intuitive understanding of this natural flow of life comes a grace and an acceptance for one's place in it, as well as for that place's limitations and inevitable transformations.[33] Act according to who you truly are, and follow the course of the Way. Rely on nothing and enjoy the world. You will know what to do.

故君子居易以俟命

Thus the Gentleman resides in the easy/changing,
And awaits [heaven's] command.[34]

Humor

It must be noted that a part of this Perennial Philosophy and a legacy of the old man's book is a lighthearted sense of humor, based in part on not taking one's self too seriously. Early on in the text, after all, we are reminded that Heaven and Earth "treat all creatures as straw dogs" (verse 5)—that is, the small straw dolls made for certain festivals and thrown into the fire or discarded once the festivities are over. This is to say that we all take part in the celebration of the

Great Transformation, but we must remember that the party is, in one sense, a masquerade, and that we should not become confused by, or attached to, the costumes. Indeed, it is the nonexistence inside of each disguise that is the lasting and great "utility" (verse 11).

It is in truly understanding this paradox of existing in nonexistence and relying on nothing that we gain a freedom that is often accompanied by the laughter of recognition expressed by the old man's disciples, Chuang Tzu and Lieh Tzu. The game of life, then, is much more amusing and played far more easily, as Lieh Tzu humorously and metaphorically wrote:

> When you gamble for tiles, you are skillful. When you gamble for your belt buckle, you begin to hesitate; and when you gamble for gold, you get confused. Your skill is the same, but you get cautious because you value something outside of yourself.
>
> —*Lieh Tzu*, Chap. 2

In Chinese folk wisdom, which is permeated by the old man's sayings, this is transmitted as the following:

自大是個臭字

"Self" and "Great" together create a "Stink,"[35]

a play on words, resonating with the old man's saying that

> If you take up studying, you increase day by day.
> If you take up the Way, you decrease day by day.
> You decrease and then decrease again.   VERSE 48

Conclusion

We read the old man's book because it is a wellspring of one of the most elevating, sophisticated, and lasting cultures in the history of the world. As such, it has been the inspiration for much of Far Eastern art, poetry, philosophy, and literature. We read the book because it takes us away from the busy and all too often unsatisfying world of business and politics, and provides entry to a Way quite removed from power-grabbing, dishonesty, and greed. But we also read it, as it has been read for millennia, for the rhythm and beauty of its phrasing and vocabulary, which often give us an astonishing satisfaction even when we are not quite sure what the old man is saying.

And this is perhaps the secret of why the book has consistently been on people's bookshelves and bedstands and in their rucksacks for nearly twenty-five centuries. There are times when we read its verses and are brought back to a moment listening to the bamboo creaking in the backyard, or watching two or three crows flying west in the early evening, or maybe catching the scent of the first real day of autumn. None of these have names or explanations. None of these "act," but we feel their profound significance and understand somehow that there are deeper measures to the world much closer to us than we are ordinarily aware of.[36]

This is the mystery of the old man's book. This is what he left us on his way through the pass.

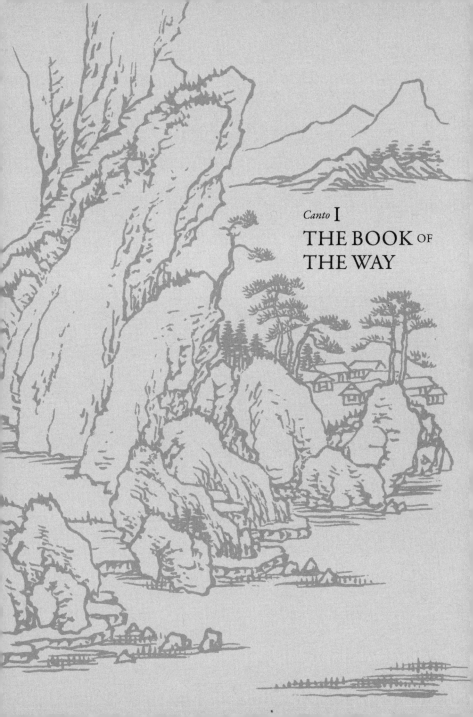

Canto I
THE BOOK OF
THE WAY

1

The Way that can be articulately described
     is not the Unchanging Way.[1]
The name that can be said out loud
     is not the Unchanging Name.
With your mouth unopened, and things left undefined,
     you stand at the beginning of the universe.
Make definitions, and you are the measure of all creation.
Thus, being forever without desire,
     you look deeply into the transcendent.
By constantly harboring desire,
     your vision is beset by all the things around you.
These two enter the world alike,
     but their names are different.
Alike, they are called profound and remote.
Profound and remote and again more so:
This is the gate to all mysteries.

Everybody understands the beautiful to be "beautiful,"
But this only creates the concept of "ugly";
Everybody understands the good to be "good,"
But this only creates the concept of "bad."[2]

There can be no existence without nonexistence;
No difficult without easy;
No long without short;
No high without low;
And without the sounds of musical instruments and
      human voices, where would
      their harmony—and cacophony—be?

Before and after only depend on which one follows first.
Therefore the sage resides in nonfabrication,[3] and
      conducts himself according to wordless teachings.
All objects in the world come into existence, but he does
      not judge them;
They are born, but he does not possess them.
The sage acts, but relies on nothing;
    He accomplishes and moves on.
    By moving on, he never has to leave.

3

Do not respect the clever,[4] and the people will not be
      induced to conflict.
Do not be impressed by hard-to-get material things, and
      the people will not be induced to covet what they
      lack and grab what is not theirs.
Do not stare at the desirable, and the people will not be
      induced to entangling thoughts.

Therefore the sage manages
      the flow of their activities like this:
   He empties their minds, but fills their stomachs;
   He weakens their willfulness,
      but strengthens their bones.
   He constantly leads the people
      toward less "knowledge" and less desire.

Thus, "masters" and "wise men" will not dare to act.
Act without fabrication, and there will be nothing you
      cannot manage.

The Way is as empty as an empty bowl,
Yet when used, it never fills.

Deep and ill-defined, it resembles the distant ancestor of
  all things.
It blunts sharp edges, unravels their tangles,
  softens their blazing light,
   and blends one with their dust.
Gentle and overflowing, it always seems to be there.
I don't know who gives it birth;
It appears to precede the creator of us all.

5

Heaven and Earth are not out to make friends;
Thus, they treat all creatures as straw dogs.[5]
The sage is not out to make friends;
Thus, he treats the people as straw dogs.
Perhaps this is something like a bellows between Heaven
    and Earth:
It is empty, but never exhausted;
It moves, and creatures are manifested endlessly.
A lot of words will get you nowhere;
Better just to stay centered.

6

The daemon of the valley does not die;
It is called the dark and mysterious female.[6]
The gate of the dark and mysterious female
Is called the root of Heaven and Earth.
It seems to exist like an unending thread;
Use it—it never wears out.

7

Heaven is everlasting; Earth, age-old.

The reason Heaven and Earth are everlasting and age-old:

> They do not live for themselves.

> Thus, they are able to endure.

Therefore the sage

> Puts himself last, but remains at the fore;

> Puts himself outside, but stays within.[7]

Is it not due to his selflessness,

That he himself is fulfilled?

8

Better than holding the cup until filled to the brim,
Is knowing when to stop.
If you continue to temper and sharpen a blade,
It will not hold its edge for long.[10]
When gold and jewels fill the hall,
Keeping them under *your* roof will be difficult.
Riding the high horse of your own wealth and position,
You will invite censure all on your own.

When you have completed some meritorious deed,
Back out and go home.
This is heaven's Way.

10

Riding the wild corporeal spirit *and* embracing the One:
Can you do this without letting one of them go?
Concentrating your *ch'i and* mastering the pliant:
Can you do this and become like a nursing child?
Cleaning off the stains from the mirror of your mind:[11]
Can you do this without streaking it yourself?
Loving the people *and* steering the country:
Can you do this without fabrication?
Opening and closing the Gate of heaven:[12]
Can you do this acting as the female?
Sending out a bright and clear wisdom in all directions:
Can you do this unconsciously?[13]

Bring things to life and nurture them,
But have no thoughts of possession.
Act without relying on anything;
Bring things along, but do not take charge.
This is the dark and mysterious virtue.

11

Thirty spokes make the nave of a wheel,
Yet it is the nonbeing
　　　at the center of the wheel that is the wheel's utility.[14]
It is the kneaded clay that fashions a pot,
Yet it is the nonexistence
　　　inside the pot that is the pot's utility.
It is the chiseling out of windows
　　　and a door that make a room,
Yet it is the nonexistence
　　　in the door and windows that is the room's utility.

Therefore, it is by existence that we set the stage,[15]
But by nonexistence that we have utility.

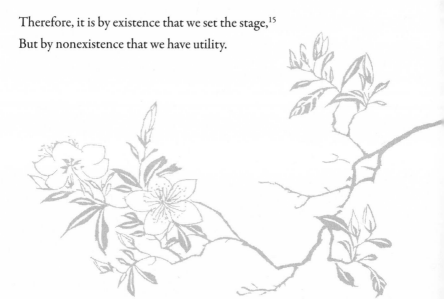

12

The five colors combined will make you blind.
The five sounds combined will make you deaf.
The five tastes combined will confuse your mouth.[16]
Whipping your horse around hunting in the fields will
        make you as crazy as a mad dog.
Valuables hard to obtain will hobble your behavior.

For this reason, the sage thinks about his stomach, but not
        about what he sees around him.
He takes the one, but passes the other by.

13

Be alarmed by either honors or disgrace.
Respect those things that pain the mind as you would
      those that pain the body.[17]

What does it mean to say that you should be alarmed by
      either honors or disgrace?
Consider honors to be of a lower order:
Be alarmed by receiving them;
Be alarmed by losing them.
This is what it means to say that
      you should be alarmed by either honors or disgrace.

What does it mean to say that
      you should respect those things that pain the mind
      as you would those that pain the body?
The reason that you have things that pain the mind is
      because you have a physical body.
If you did not have a physical body,
      how would you have things that pain the mind?

Thus, a person who respects his body *and* rules an empire
May indeed be entrusted with the empire;
A person who loves his body and rules the empire
May indeed be depended upon to rule.

14

You stare at it fixedly, but do not see it.

It is called Dim.

You listen to it carefully, but do not hear it.[18]

It is called Indistinct.

You touch it, but feel nothing.

It is called Vague.

These three cannot be investigated with clarity,

And mixed up like rushing water, act as one.

From above, it is not clear;

From below, it is not dark.

As continuous as an unending cord, it cannot be named,

And returns to No-Thing.

This is called the form of No-Form,

Or the shape of No-Thing.[19]

It is called vacant and abstracted.

When you approach it, you will not see its head;

When you follow it, you will not see its behind.

Take tight grasp of the Way of antiquity

And you will lead present existence as you would a horse.

Being able to understand the

  Ancient Beginning with all of your senses,

Is called the beginning thread of the Way.

15

The men who practiced the Way effectively in the past
Were unfathomable and beyond description;
You could not get a sense of their depth
And although you could not get a sense of their depth,
I will persist, and try to create a picture of them:

Hesitating, like crossing a stream in winter;
Wavering, like fearing demons with clubs on all sides;
Respectful, like being a guest;
Pliant, like ice about to melt;
Unpretentious, like rough lumber;
In plain view, like a valley;
Mixing and mingling, like muddy water.[20]

Who can gradually clarify muddy water with tranquility?
Who can gradually bring life into
the complacent with activity?
Those who care for the Way
as they would a child carried on their back.

Do not wish to be filled to the brim.
Exactly because they are not filled to the brim,
When worn out like old clothing,
they are renewed yet again.

16

Bring yourself steadily to absolute emptiness.
Preserve your tranquility in a careful fashion,
      like a slowly walking horse.
All creatures are brought into being one after another,
But with this, I perceive their return.

Listen, creatures are of countless varieties,
But each returns to its root.
Returning to its root is called tranquility,
And this is called returning to its naturally given course.[21]
Returning to its naturally given course is
      called the Unchanging;
Understanding the Unchanging is
      called the bright and clear.
If you do not understand the Unchanging,[22]
You will be doing things in the dark,
      and this is ill-omened.

If you know the Unchanging, you will have latitude;
Having latitude is being open to all.
Being open to all is being kingly;
Being kingly is being as broad as heaven.
Being as broad as heaven is the Way,
And the Way transcends time.
In this way, you will be without danger
      until your body sinks beneath the sea of existence.

17

The greatest superior is he
>   whose inferiors know only that he is there.
The next in line is he
>   who is held in familial affection and praised.
The next is he
>   who is feared as a demon armed with cudgels.
The lowest is he who is regarded as a lightweight.

When a man does not sufficiently stand by his words,
>   there will be no standing by words anywhere.

Think broadly and value your words as wealth.[23]
Finish your work, accomplish what you set your hand to,
>   and the people will call you a natural.

18

When the Great Way is abandoned, conscious
        sympathy and "correct" behavior will be at hand.
When masters of wisdom[24] and quick wit appear,
        great hypocrisy will be at hand.
When the six family relationships[25] are not in harmony,
        filial piety and loving upbringing will be at hand.
When the state is in confusion and its vision is dim,
        "sincere and loyal" retainers will be at hand.

19

Cut off saintliness as a knife would cut a thread, throw
    away wisdom as you would dust from a dustpan,
And the people's preparedness for life
    will increase a hundredfold.
Cut off human-heartedness and
    throw away ornamental conduct,[26]
And the people will do a direct turnaround to filial piety
    and a nurturing heart.
Cut off ingeniousness and throw away gain,
And burglars and armed bandits will not be at hand.

These three considered simply as general patterns
    will be insufficient.
Therefore I must attach something concrete to hold on to:
    Visibly demonstrate a simplicity as unadorned as white
        thread, and embrace a candidness as plain as bark.[27]
    Make less of yourself and reduce greed.

Leave off studying with your head in your hands,[28]
  and you will not be obsessed about what to do next.
How much divergence is there between
  "Yes, sir!" and "As you please"?
How much divergence
  between the attractive and the not so attractive?[29]
It's not that you should not fear what other people dread;
But it's all as entangled as a thicket and,
  sadly, you'll never get even halfway through.[30]

The majority of people are bright and pleased:
  As though guests at a great feast,[31]
  As though climbing up a high platform from
  which to look out in spring.
I alone am moored like a boat,
  with no portents of moving on;
Like a suckling child who has not yet smiled.[32]
Loaded down and tired,
  it seems that I have no place to go home.
The majority of people all have more than
  enough under their roofs,

While I alone seem to have forgotten
    all my goods along the way.
Do I, alas, have the mind of a fool?

Ahh, undiscriminating and in the dark,[33]
While the average man is sunshine bright.
I alone am as dim as dusk,[34]
While the average man sees everything in detail.
I alone have a fenced-in mind,
Like a shallow and irresolute sea,
Like a high-pitched wind that never stops.
The common run of men all have something to do,
But I alone am disordered and indiscriminate,
    resembling a hayseed from out of town.
I alone am unlike others,
And value being nourished at the Mother's breast.

21

The manifested forms contained within the Great Virtue
      only follow along behind the Way.
That which is considered the real existence of the Way is
      now abstract, now dim.

Now dim, now abstract: within it is form.
Now abstract, now dim: within it real existence is at hand.
Darkly cavernous and like a moonless night:
      within it is the quintessence.[35]
This quintessence is the extreme truth:
      within it is the stamp of proof.[36]

From ancient times until the recent,
      it identifies itself without fail,
And thus we examine the beginnings of all things.
How do I know this matter of the beginnings of all things?
It's right here.

22

That which is twisted will remain whole.[37]

That which bends will become straight.[38]

That which is hollowed out like a melon will be filled to
the brim.

That which is torn like cloth will be re-cut and made anew.

Having less, you can receive;

Having more, you become confused.

Therefore, the wise man

Embraces the One,

and becomes the model for all under heaven;

Does not make himself seen,

and therefore is as bright as the sun and moon;

Does not consider himself good,

and therefore is a pattern for all;

Does not denigrate others to make himself look good,

and therefore gets the credit;[39]

Does not make himself like the arrogant grip of a spear,

and therefore becomes a staff of support.[40]

Listen, it is simply that he does not contend.

Thus no one under heaven can contend with him.

The saying of the ancients,

"The twisted will remain whole"—

How could these be empty words?

In truth, it will remain whole,

and will return to the Source.[41]

23

It is natural to have few words.[42]
Thus, the whirlwind that blows things around as though
      they were bugs, does not last the morning.
Neither does the sudden storm last the day.
Who is it that concocts such things?
Heaven and Earth.
But Heaven and Earth cannot sustain them for long.
How, then, could Man?

Therefore, he who follows the Way in
      what he puts his hand to,
Will be included among the men of the Way
And will be included among men of virtue;
In losing the Way and its virtue,
      he will be included among those of similar loss.[43]

Those who gather under the gate of
      the Way are in turn happily received by the Way.
Those who gather under the gate of
      virtue are in turn happily received by virtue.
Those who gather under the gate of loss
      are in turn happily received by loss.

When one does not sufficiently stand by his words,
A general loss of faith will be at hand.

24

If you are up on tiptoes, you will
      not stand with confidence.
If you move along straddling the road, you will
      be unable to put one foot in front of the other.
If you make yourself seen, you will not be illustrious.
If you consider yourself right, you will
      not be taken as a model.
If you denigrate others, you will get no credit.
If you consider yourself the grip of a spear, you will
      never become a staff of support.

Those who abide in the Way
Call such things
      "leftover food" or "warts on your behavior."
Thus, those who possess the Way will be found elsewhere.

25

BUSINESS REPLY MAIL
FIRST-CLASS MAIL   PERMIT NO. 11494   BOSTON MA

POSTAGE WILL BE PAID BY ADDRESSEE

SHAMBHALA PUBLICATIONS
PO BOX 170358
BOSTON MA 02117-9812

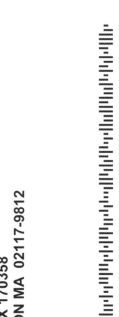

SHAMBHALA PUBLICATIONS

If you'd like to receive a copy of our latest catalogue of books and audios, please fill out and return this card. It's easy—the postage is already paid!

Or, if you'd prefer, you can e-mail us at CustomerCare@shambhala.com, sign up online at www.shambhala.com/newsletter, or call toll-free (888) 424-2329.

NAME

ADDRESS

CITY / STATE / ZIP / COUNTRY

E-MAIL

And by also giving us your e-mail address, you'll automatically be signed up to receive news about new releases, author events, and special offers!

There is something mingled and ungraspable
     as bubbling water, and yet quite complete;
It exists[44] before Heaven and Earth.[45]
It is quiet and tranquil; empty and at rest.
It stands on its own, and cannot be altered;
Manifests itself in all things, and is never idle.[46]
You could consider it
     the nursing mother of all under heaven.
I myself do not know its name,
     but for starters, call it the Way.
Pushed to make up a name, you could call it Great.
The Great is said to flow out and beyond;
Flowing out and beyond is said to journey far away;
To journey far away is said to return.

Thus, the Way is Great,
Heaven is Great,
Earth is Great,
And the king is also Great.[47]
For all in existence, there are four Greats,
And the king takes his place as one of them.
Man follows the flow of the Earth.
Earth follows the flow of Heaven.
Heaven follows the flow of the Way.
The Way follows the flow of the Of-Itself-So.

The heavy fabricates the root of the light.
The tranquil fabricates command of the flurried.

Therefore the sage puts one foot
     in front of the other the entire day,[48]
   But never leaves his heavy pack behind.
   Though there may be glorious sights at hand,
   His course remains high and detached,
     as smooth as the flight of a swallow.
   How will a lord of ten thousand chariots fool
     with his empire as though
     he himself had nothing to lose?

Act lightly and you lose your rootedness.
Act in a flurried way and you lose your command.

27

Auspicious traveling leaves neither ruts nor tracks.
Auspicious words have neither flaws nor points for blame.
Auspicious calculation needs neither bamboo markers
      nor receipts.
The auspiciously shut has neither bolt nor key,
      but cannot be opened.
The auspiciously fastened uses neither rope nor binder,
      but cannot be untied.

Therefore the sage
    Always saves men from their mistakes in a goodly fashion,
    And thus no one is thrown overboard;
    Always saves things from their flaws in a skillful way,
    And thus none are tossed away.
This is called doubling and tripling your clarity.
In this way the adroit are the teachers of the clumsy,
And the clumsy are a wealth of raw material for the adroit.
If you do not treasure your teacher
      or show kindness to your raw material,
You will be shortsighted
      though you have the wisdom to predict the rain.
This is called the pivotal mystery.

28

If you know the male but preserve the female,
You will effect a mountain stream[49] for all under heaven.[50]
Effecting a mountain stream for all under heaven,
You will stay close to the Unchanging virtue[51]
And be restored to the state of a suckling child.

If you know the bright but preserve the dark,
You will effect a model for all under heaven.
Effecting a model for all under heaven,
You will not run counter to the Unchanging virtue
And will be restored to That-Without-Limit.

If you know the flourishing but preserve the retiring,
You will effect a valley[52] for all under heaven.
Effecting a valley for all under heaven,
Your Unchanging virtue will not be lacking
And you will be restored to a state of plain,
        unfinished wood.

When plain, unfinished wood is broken up into pieces,
The pieces may be fashioned into utensils.[53]
If the "wise man" uses these,
        they will be fashioned into bureaucrats.
For this reason,
        the Great Preparer of things does not break them up.

29

When a man wishes to take the world and make
        something of it,
I perceive that this will only end in failure.
The world is an instrument regulated by the gods,
And cannot be fabricated into something else.
He who tries to do this will damage it.
He who tries to grasp it will lose it.

Thus, as for the creatures of this world,
    There are those who step forward,
        and those who follow;
    There are those who breathe through their noses,
        and those who breathe through their mouths.
    There are those as strong as the sting of a wasp,
        and those as delicate as a sickly sheep.
    There are those who are thrown down,
        and those who fall down on their own.

Therefore the sage
    Avoids the extreme,
    Avoids the arrogant and self-willed,
    And avoids the excessive.

30

He who would wholeheartedly help
      the ruler of men by means of the Way
Will not use military weapons
      to force himself on the world.
In putting his hands to things,
      he prefers returning to the fundamental Way.
Wherever troops bivouac,
      thorny shrubs and spiny brambles grow.
After the clashes of great armies,
      years of empty fields and hungry mouths
      will inevitably be at hand.

The man adroit at government only brings affairs to
      fruition as fruit will grow on trees.
He does not dare to grasp in order to strengthen.
Bringing affairs to fruition,
      he does not make much of himself.
Bringing affairs to fruition, he does not contend.
Bringing affairs to fruition,
      he does not look down on others.
Bringing affairs to fruition,
      he does so only when it can't be helped.[54]
Bringing affairs to fruition, he does not force others.

After creatures reach their peak,
      they begin to grow bent and old.
This is said not to be following the Way.
Those who do not follow the Way soon come to an end.

31

Listen, well-polished weapons are inauspicious tools;
All creatures consistently back away from them.
Thus, a man who possesses the Way

    will not have them around.
When the Gentleman is at home, he keeps them at his left;[55]
But when in use, he keeps them at his right.[56]

But weapons are inauspicious tools,
And they are not the tools of the Gentleman.[57]
He uses them only when it can't be helped,
And considers tranquility and simplicity

    to be the highest good.[58]
Victory he does not find beautiful,
For to do so would be to enjoy killing others.
And listen, the man who enjoys killing others
Will find his ambitions thwarted in this world.

In auspicious matters, you honor the left;
In inauspicious matters, you honor the right.
A company commander will occupy the left;
The commander-in-chief will occupy the right.
Which is to say that their formation is

    proper to that of a funeral.

When many people are killed
We shed tears in pity and grief.
For victory in battle, we take a stance proper to funeral rites.

32

The Way is unchanging and is without name.[59]
Though its unvarnished state may seem of little account,
It is subordinate to nothing in this world.
If lords and kings were able to keep it in store,
The Ten Thousand Things would surely follow their lead.

Heaven and Earth mutually unite,
     and sweet dew descends.
Without people's command,
     it falls equally of its own accord.

When you begin to divide and arrange, names are at hand;
And when names are already at hand,
You should know that it's time to stop.
It is by knowing when to stop that
     you will not tread on dangerous ground.

To give a comparison, the Way's existence in the world
Is like rivers and streams flowing into inlets and seas.

33

He who knows others may have knowledge
      enough to predict the rain,
But he who knows himself
      will see with the clarity of the sun and moon.[60]
He who is victorious over others has strength,
But he who is victorious over himself
      will have the potency of a swarm of bees.

He who knows how to stop with what is sufficient is
      rich with his own house and fields,
And he who puts one foot in front of the other with
      strength will have resolution.
He who does not lose his place will stay long,
And he who dies but is not forgotten will be long-lived.[61]

The Way drifts buoyantly, now left, now right.[62]
The Ten Thousand Things rely on it,
    and are born without fanfare.
It does good work, but does not hold on to fame.
It clothes and nourishes the Ten Thousand Things,
    but does not assume to be their master.

As it is always without desire,
    you might name it the Insignificant.
The Ten Thousand Things return to it,
    but do not consider it their master.
You could give it a name, and fashion it the Great,
But it does not consider itself great.
Thus it is able to achieve its magnitude.

35

If you shackle[63] yourself to the Great Form,[64]
And walk about in the world,
You may walk about without harm,[65]
And with security, peace, and ease.

If there are stringed instruments and dumplings,
The traveler passing through will stop;
But what comes from the mouth of the Way
Is like thin soup without taste.[66]
You may gaze at it fixedly, but there's little to see;
You may listen to it intently, but there's little to hear;
You may use it all you like, and it will never be used up.[67]

36

If you wish to draw in your wings,
You must momentarily stretch them out.
If you wish to weaken something,
You must momentarily make it strong.
If you wish to bring something lower,
You must momentarily lift it up.
If you wish to grasp something,
You must momentarily give it up.
This is called
    "the something hidden in the brightness of day."
The soft and weak
    will be victorious over the hard and strong.

Fish should not be taken from their deep pools;
The country's sharp weapons and clever administrators
    should not be shown to the people.

37

The Way never acts,
Yet no act is left undone.[68]
If lords and kings were able to maintain this,
The Ten Thousand Things would transform on their own.
If, once transforming, desire were to arise,
I would calm this desire with an unvarnished simplicity
        that has no name.

Listen, with this unvarnished simplicity without a name
There will be no desires.
Without desires, there will be peace,
And all under heaven will be settled on its own.

Canto II
THE BOOK OF VIRTUE

38

The highest virtue does not act virtuously;
Therefore, virtue is at hand.
The lowest virtue won't let go of virtue;
Therefore, it has none.

The highest virtue does not act according to form,
So nothing is fabricated.
The lowest virtue acts according to form,
So everything is fabricated.
The highest human-heartedness acts according to form,
Yet nothing is fabricated.[69]
The highest righteousness acts according to form,
So everything is fabricated.
The highest etiquette acts according to form,
And if there is no proper response,
Rolls up its sleeves and presses on.

Thus, lose the Way, and virtue will come up from behind;
Lose virtue, and human-heartedness will come up
        from behind;
Lose human-heartedness,
        and righteousness will come up from behind.
Lose righteousness, and you'll get good manners.

Listen, a person with good manners
Is thin on loyalty and standing by his word,[70]
And this is the headwaters of disorder.
Consciousness before action
Creates the flower of the Way
And is the beginning of circuitous thinking.

Therefore, the man of character
Will sit down with the grounded,
But will not associate with the light-headed;
Will sit down with the fruit,
But will not associate with the flower.
Thus, he avoids the one, and takes the other.

39

Of those who obtained

the One along the way in ancient times:
Heaven obtained the One, and became transparent;
Earth obtained the One, and became pacified;[71]
The spirits obtained the One, and

were imbued with the essential mystery of things;
The valleys obtained the One, and were filled to the brim;
The Ten Thousand Things obtained the One,

and sprouted with life;[72]
Lords and kings obtained the One,

and divined how to make the world correct.
It was the One that guided them along.

If Heaven were not transparent,

I'm afraid it would soon be rent like cloth.

If Earth were not pacified,

I'm afraid it would soon begin to shake.

If the spirits were not imbued with

the essential mystery of things,

I'm afraid they would soon not bother to exert themselves.

If the valleys were not filled to the brim,

I'm afraid they would soon be dried up.

If the Ten Thousand Things did not sprout with life,

I'm afraid they would soon become parched and wither.

If lords and kings were not respected and on high,

I'm afraid they would soon stumble and fall.[73]

Thus, that which is of little value creates

the foundation for that which is treasured,

And that which is low creates

a bedrock for that which is high.

Therefore, lords and kings call

themselves orphans, widowers, and menials.

Is this not making what is of little value the foundation?

Is this not so?

Thus, though you may often be awarded words of praise,

you will have no honor.

Do not wish to jangle like jewels;

Rather, resonate like rocks and stones.[74]

40

Return is the movement of the Way;
The weak and flexible is the function of the Way.[75]

The Ten Thousand Things of the world are born from
      existence;
Existence is born from nonexistence.[76]

41

When the best kind of educated Gentleman
        hears of the Way,
He braces himself, puts effort into it,
        and behaves accordingly.
When the middling kind hears of the Way,
He thinks maybe it exists, but maybe it doesn't.
When the lowest type hears of the Way,
He gives a belly laugh.[77]
If he did not laugh,
It would not suffice to be considered the Way.

Thus, there are these lodestar sayings:

The Way, as bright as the sun and moon, is like the
darkness before dawn.

When the Way advances, it seems to be retreating.

The Way that subdues and makes all things
even seems to be tangled and ambiguous.

The highest virtue seems like
the empty mouth of a valley.

That which is immaculate seems muddy and unclear.

An open and unblocked virtue seems unapproachable.

Established virtue seems provisional.

The rock-solid truth seems
as changeable as flowing water.

The great square of the Earth has no corners.

A great vessel is made over time.[78]

A great sound has a rare voice.

A great form is without shape.[79]

The Way is hidden and without an identifying name.[80]

Listen, it is only the Way that attends to
the intrinsic value of things well,[81]
and then brings them to completion.

42

The Way gives birth to the One;[82]
The One gives birth to the Two;[83]
The Two gives birth to the Three;[84]
The Three gives birth to the Ten Thousand Things.
The Ten Thousand Things carry
      the Yin and enfold the Yang;
Kneading them gently, they create harmony.

What people dislike is to be orphaned, widowed, or to
      become menials.
Still, kings and princes account themselves as such.
Thus at times, creatures suffer decrease,[85]
      and yet increase.[86]
At times they increase, and yet suffer decrease.

What people exhort,[87]
I do as well:
The strong and self-assertive will not achieve
      the death they would like.
This teaching I would make the keeper of the sacred fire.

43

The softest in the world dominate the
      hardest just as you would whip forward a horse.
That without form or substance[88] enters
      where there is no space at all.
By this I know beyond a doubt
      the fulfillment of nonfabrication.
Wordless teaching, the fulfillment of nonfabrication:
In this world there are few who can grasp these.

44

Your reputation or your physical self:

     which do you see as your very life?

Your physical self or your capital:

     which is better?

To pick up something along the way or to lose something:

     which is more inductive to pain?

For these reasons, if you desire something excessively,

     you will invariably have great expenses;

If you store many things away,

     you will invariably lose things by the pile.

If you clearly know what is sufficient,

     you will not be embarrassed;

If you know when to stop,

     you will not stand on shaky ground.

Thus, you will be able to continue for a long time.

45

Great accomplishment seems lacking,
  But its use never fails.
A bowl filled to the top seems empty,
  But its use never comes to an end.

The perfectly straight seems crooked;
Great skill seems like bungling;
Mellifluous speech seems tongue-tied.[89]

Flurried movement defeats the cold;
Tranquility defeats the heat.
Clarity and tranquility make the world impartial.

46

When the Way is at hand in the world,
Running horses are led back to the fields to create manure.
When the Way is not in the world,
Generations of horses are born
    within the borders of the state.

There is no disaster greater
    than not knowing what is enough.
There is no fault greater than wanting to obtain more.
Thus, the sufficiency of knowing what is sufficient
Is unchangingly sufficient!

Know the world without leaving your door;[90]
Observe heaven's Way
         without peering through your window.[91]
When you go out and travel farther and farther away,
What you know for certain diminishes.

Therefore the sage
    Does not step out, but knows with certainty;
    Does not look around, but identifies things;
    Does not fabricate, but things come to fruition.

48

If you take up studying, you increase day by day.
If you take up the Way, you decrease day by day.[92]
You decrease and then decrease again.
In this way, you reach the point of nonfabrication:
Nothing is fabricated, but there is nothing left undone.[93]

Taking up the affairs of the world
Is always done without meddling.
If there is meddling,
It will not be sufficient to accomplish the job.

49

The sage does not have an unchanging mind.

He makes the mind of the people his own.

He is good to those who are good,

And good to those who are not good.

Thus, his virtue is good.

He stands by his words to those who stand by their words,

And he stands by his words to those who do not.

Thus, his virtue is reliable.

The sage resides in the world,

Harmonizes with it, and for the sake of the world,

  flows in convergence with its heartbeat.[94]

People all give him their eyes and their ears,

And he treats them as he would laughing children.

50

We come out into life, and go back into death.
Three out of ten follow along after life;
Three out of ten follow along after death;[95]
And another three out of ten are given life,
      but by their activities march off after death.

Listen, why should this be?
It is because they are too strongly attached to life.

I have heard it generally said that
      a man who is good at taking care of his life
Will travel hill and dale,
      but not encounter wild horned buffalos[96] or tigers;
He will enter a battlefield,
      but not put on protective armor.
The wild buffalo finds no place to thrust its horns,
The tiger finds no place to sink its claws,
And soldiers find no place to strike with their blades.

Now listen, why is this?
It is because for him, there is no dangerous place.[97]

51

The Way gives them life.

Virtue gives them sustenance.

Color and shape give them form.

Energy gives them completion.

Therefore, the Ten Thousand Things

Respect the Way and treasure virtue.

Respecting the Way and treasuring virtue:

No one commands them to do this;

It is always just Of-Itself-So.

Thus, the Way gives them life,

And virtue gives them sustenance.

Both give them long life, and raise them as though
       bringing them through childbirth.

Both give them refuge, and keep them from harm;

Both nourish them and provide them with cover;[98]

Both give them life, but do not possess them.

Both act, but rely on nothing;

Both give them long life, but do not direct their affairs.

Both are called the dark and but dimly seen virtue.

All beneath heaven has a beginning;
You could consider it the nursing mother of the world.
When you have grasped who that mother is,
You will also clearly know who her children are.
When you clearly know who the children are,
You will, in turn, sustain the mother.
Thus, you will not be in danger to your very last gasp.
Plug up the leaks[99] as you would a wall with mud,
Close up the gates[100] with a bar,
And to the end of your life you will not feel
        the squeeze of your endeavors.

Open up the leaks,
Let them go to work,
And to the end of your life, nothing will be of any help.
Observing the infinitesimal is called
        the illumination of the sun and moon;
Maintaining the soft and malleable is called
        the strength of the wasp's sting.
If you make use of a light as intense as a fire
And return again to its illumination,
Life's disasters will be gone and forgotten.
This is called the practice of the Unchanging.

53

If I should allow myself even a small portion of knowledge,
When putting one foot
      in front of the other on the Great Way,
I fear that I would only wander off a twisting bypath.
The Great Way is extraordinarily broad,
      like a bow when drawn,
But the people favor narrow ways.

Though the courts are swept clean of honesty,
The fields are choked with reedy weeds,
And the warehouses are quite empty;
Beautifully patterned robes are worn,
Sharp swords are fastened to sashes,
Food and drink are consumed to surfeit,
And valuables and capital are at hand in excess.
This is called the grandeur of thieves.
It is emphatically not the Way.

54

He who is well set up, like a brush held erect,
      will not be pulled away.
He who embraces it[101] with both hands,
      will not have it slip away;
Thus, his descendents will not pause in performing
      sacrifices to his spirit.

If you cultivate this for your own person
      as you would sweep and prune,
Its virtue will be pure.
If you cultivate this in the same way for your household,
Its virtue will be plentiful.
If you cultivate this among those in your village,
Its virtue will be long lasting.
If you cultivate this among those
      within your provincial borders,
Its virtue will be like vessels
      filled with an abundant harvest.
If you cultivate this with all under heaven,
Its virtue will go everywhere.[102]

Thus, you should contemplate
      a household as a household,
You should contemplate
      those in a village as those in a village,
You should contemplate a country as a country.
And all under heaven will be
      contemplated as all under heaven.
How do I know that this is so for all under heaven?
I know from this very order of things.

55

He who holds on to virtue sincerely and deeply within
Can be compared to a newborn child.[103]
Wasps, scorpions, vipers, and other snakes
    will not sting or bite him;
Fierce beasts will not reach for him with their claws;
And birds of prey will not strike him with curled talons.
His bones will be pliant, his sinews will be soft,
    and yet his grasp will be unyielding.
He does not yet know the conjoining of male and
    female parts, but his own stands right up.
His pure spirit has arrived like an arrow
    piercing the earth.[104]
He may scream like a tiger the entire day, but his throat
    will not become parched.
His harmony, too, is at its best.[105]

Knowing harmony is called the Unchanging;[106]
Knowing the Unchanging is called illumination.
To make life overflow its limits
    is said to be bad luck in the guise of good.[107]
For the mind to put *ch'i* at its beck and call
    is said to be forceful.

When creatures reach their peak,
    they become deformed and distorted.
This is said not to be following the Way.
Those who do not follow the Way, soon come to an end.

56

The knowing do not speak.[108]
Those speaking do not know.

Plug up the leaks as you would a wall with mud,
Close up the gates with a bar.[109]
Blunt your pointiness,
Unravel your tangles,
Soften your blazing light,
Become as the dust raised by a herd of passing deer.
This is called the dark identity.[110]

With such a person, no family intimacy can be obtained,
But neither can distance or estrangement.
From him, advantage cannot be obtained,
But neither can hurt or harm.
He cannot be valued,
Nor considered of no account.[111]
Thus he is treasured by all under heaven.

57

Manage the flow of the state with impartiality;
Use the military in an unexpected manner;
Take the world as you would a trophy from a vanquished
      foe without even putting your hand to it.
How do I know this can be so?
From this very order of things:
When fear and loathing proliferate in the world,
The people will become increasingly destitute.
When the people have an abundance
      of sharp weapons and clever leaders,
The state will become increasingly dusky and dark.
When men are filled with stratagems and cunning,
Strange and eccentric objects will appear with fecundity.
When laws and commands are
      drummed up time and again,
More and more burglars and muggers will be at hand.

Thus, the sage says,
   I do nothing creative, and the people change of
      themselves;[112]
   I am fond of restraint in conflict, and the people
      become impartial on their own;
   I put my hand to nothing,
      and the people prosper by themselves;
   I desire nothing, and the people have
      unvarnished simplicity on their own.[113]

58

If the affairs of the state are gloomy and troubled,
The people will be confined like water unable to flow;
Yet when the affairs of state are clear and exacting,
The people will find themselves lacking.[114]

Disaster hinges on good fortune,
While blessings from the gods lie concealed within
      distorted circumstances.
Who knows when either reaches its limit?[115]
There is nothing that does not eventually lean one way or
      the other.
Correctness again creates eccentricity;
Good again creates the suspicious.[116]
Men have no clear vision of their way,
As has been since days long ago.

For this reason, the sage
    Is four-cornered, but does not cut with sharp edges;
    Is a sharp straight crease, but does not tear;
    Has straightened what was once bent, but does not
      stretch things out self-indulgently;
    Is as bright as a blazing fire, but does not flash or flare.

59

For directing the flow of human affairs,
        and offering your hand to heaven's,
There is nothing like frugality, as you would
        put grain carefully away in a storehouse.
Listen, only such frugality
Is said to be quick obeisance to the Way.
Quick obeisance is said to accumulate virtue,
        layer upon layer.
Accumulating virtue in this way is exactly like
        donning a helmet and becoming unbeatable.
Being unbeatable,
You will know no limits.
Knowing no limits,
You will have the country in your hand.

Having the nursing mother of the country in your hands,
You will last long into old age,
        with long white hair and a cane.
This is called having deep roots and strong radicles.[117]
It is the Way of long life and unwavering vision.

60

Directing the flow of affairs of a large country
Is like cooking a small fresh fish.[118]

When going out and confronting the world with the Way
The gods and demons are
     no longer like thunder and lightning.[119]
And it's not just that they're
     no longer like thunder and lightning,
But they can
     no longer harm people with their slings and arrows.
And it's not just that they can
     no longer harm people with their slings and arrows,
But the sage cannot harm them in like way either.

Listen, when none of these can do harm this way,
Virtues return home one after another.

61

A large country resembles the lower reaches of a river:
Here, all under heaven meet and mix
        like the alternate collars of a robe,
And this is the female of the world.
The female constantly overcomes
        the male by means of peace and noncontention;
With peace and noncontention,
        it takes the lower position.
Thus, if a large country places itself in a lower position
        than a small country,
It will take that small country like a victor in war
        takes the left ear of the vanquished as a trophy.

If a small country takes a position beneath a large country,
It will take that large country in the same way.
Thus, there are cases when you may take others
      by putting yourself in the lower position,
And cases when you may take others by
      having been in the lower position in the first place.

Large countries do not go beyond wanting to
      unite men in one political entity and to lay them in
      stock as they might grains from the fields.
Small countries want nothing more than
      to enter into the service of large countries.

Listen, if both get what they desire,
The large country should happily
      put itself in the lower position.

62

The Way is the storehouse and kitchen[120] of
      the Ten Thousand Things.
It is a treasure for the good man who is a blessing for all,
And a place of support for the bad man, as it would carry
      him on its back as though he were a child.

Beautiful words can bring you respect in the marketplace;
Beautiful behavior can bring men to your side.
As for a man with nothing good about him,
Would you throw him away
      like tossing out trash with both hands?[121]

Thus, when a new emperor is established,
When the Three Ministers[122] are set in place,
Though you may offer up large, elaborately decorated
      pieces of jade with both hands, and precede these
      with chariots drawn by four horses,
This is nothing like kneeling
      in the dirt and proposing the Way.[123]

Why did the men of old treasure this Way?
Didn't they say that those who seek it out
      will pick it up along the way,
And that those who have been caught like fish in the
      nets of crime will be pardoned and given new life?
Thus, it makes all under heaven treasure it.

63

Act without fabrication.
Do the job without putting your hand to it.
Experience the delicious without tasting.

Large, small, many, few—
Return another's spitefully turning his back
    on you with virtue.

Map out a plan for the difficult while it is yet easy to
    change, like a chameleon's colors.
Do something with the big, while it is still small and
    vaguely formed.

The difficult things in the world
    are invariably fashioned from the easy.
The great affairs under heaven
    are invariably fashioned from the small.

Therefore the sage,
    In the end, does not work on the large.
Thus, the large becomes realized.

Listen, there are few who will stand by
    their words after lightly giving assent.
What appears to be too easy will invariably be too difficult.
Therefore the sage has doubts and gets ready for difficulties.
Thus, in the end, there are no difficulties at all.

That which is settled and calm is easy
    to hold in your hands.
That which has not yet manifested omens or
    signs is easy to plan for with no one the wiser.
That which is fragile is easy to crack.
That still in bits and pieces is easy to scatter
    like chips of bamboo.
Take care of things while they are not yet at hand.
Manage the flow of things
    while they are not yet in disarray.

A tree big enough to put your arms around
Sprouts from a seedling as fine as a hair.
A tower of nine stories
Goes bottom to top from continuous piles of earth.
A walk of a thousand *li*[124]
Begins beneath your feet.
He who acts on something, breaks it.[125]
He who fetters something, loses it.
For this reason, the sage
    Does not fabricate, and thus breaks nothing;
    Does not fetter, and thus loses nothing.

People follow along with their affairs,
Which unfailingly collapse as completion nears.
If they were as sincere in the end
        as they were in the beginning,
There would be no collapsing at all.
Therefore the sage

   Desires to have no desires,

   And does not treasure capital difficult to obtain.

   He studies how not to study,

   And turns back where many men go too far.
In this way he assists the Ten Thousand Things
        to be Of-Themselves-So,
But is not eager to concoct anything himself.[126]

65

The men of old who did well with the Way
Did not thereby illuminate the people.
Rather, they used it to keep them thinking in circles.
The current affairs of the people are difficult to manage
Because they have too much "wisdom."
Thus, using "wisdom" to manage the flow of the state
Is piracy of the state.
Managing the flow of the state
        without this kind of wisdom
Is the state's good fortune.

He who understands these two clearly
Has understood the law of where to stop with thought.
Constant knowledge of this law
Is called the dark and mysterious virtue.
The dark and mysterious virtue runs so deep, so distant!
With it, all creatures return.[127]
In this way—stepping back—they arrive at
        the great order of things.[128]

66

There is a reason why the great flowing rivers
      and the ocean can make themselves
      kings of the myriad mountain streams:
It is because they are well below them.
Thus, they are able to make themselves
      kings of the myriad mountain streams.
For this reason, if you wish to be above the people,
You must invariably say that you are below them.
If you wish to be ahead of the people,
You must invariably place yourself
      to follow them up from behind.

For this reason, the sage
   Takes his place above,
      but the people do not feel him to be heavy baggage;
   Takes his place in front,
      but the people do not consider him an obstruction.
For this reason, all under heaven enjoy reverencing him,
      but never feel cramped or importuned.
It is because he does not contend with others
That none under heaven can contend with him.

67

All under heaven declare that my Way is great,
      but it resembles something less worthy.[129]
Listen, it's only great
Because it doesn't look that way.
If it had such a resemblance,
How faint it would have been, and for so long!

I myself have three treasures at hand;
I keep a firm grasp on them, and protect them
      as I would a child carried on my back.
The first, I say, is nurturing love.
The second, I say, is unpretentiousness.
The third, I say, is not pushing myself ahead in the world.
Because of nurturing love,
      you are capable of courage that flows forth;
Because of unpretentiousness,
      you are capable of being expansive;
Because of not pushing yourself ahead in the world,

You are capable of having the stature of an elder
    among people of ability.
If you put nurturing love aside,
    and would still have gushing courage;
If you put unpretentiousness aside,
    and would still be expansive;
If you put following along behind aside,
    and would still be in the fore;
You will turn to white bones and desiccated flesh.

Listen, with nurturing love,
If you are brought into conflict,
    you will overcome the opposition.
If you will maintain this love, you will be firm.
When heaven is going to intervene,
It protects you unexpectedly with nurturing love.

68

The man who makes himself a good warrior[130]
    does not stride fiercely forward with a spear.
The man good in battle will repress all anger.
The man good at defeating his opponent
    will not clash with him directly.
The man good at using others
    will put himself in a low position.
This is said to be the virtue of noncontending.
It is said to be the use of other men's strength.
It is said to be making a companion of heaven,
    as if offering it a cup of wine.
In ancient times, this was paramount.[131]

69

There is a saying for the use of weapons:
    Do not be eager to act as the host; rather,
        act as the guest.
    Do not be eager to advance an inch; rather,
        step back a foot.
This is said to be moving forward without doing so;
Striking and retreating without extending your elbow;
Seizing your opponent without a weapon,
And taking over while having no opponent at all.

There is no greater disaster
        than making light of your opponent;
Making light of your opponent almost always
        results in losing your treasures
        as easily as leaves fall from the trees.
Thus, when opponents meet with raised weapons,
The one who laments the fight will win.

70

My words are wonderfully easy to understand;
They are wonderfully easy to follow step by step.
But no one under heaven is
     capable of understanding them;
Nor can they follow them step by step.
Such words have a shrine for their guiding spirit;
Such actions have a lord who gives the orders.

Listen, people have no understanding whatsoever,
And so they do not understand me.
Those who understand me are few;
Those who follow my style are quite rare.
For this reason, the sage
    Covers himself with rough clothes of animal fur,
        and holds the stringed jewels close to his chest.

71

Knowing that you do not know
  rests above the high-water mark.
Thinking that you know when you don't know,[132]
  you are sick enough to be confined in bed.
Listen, just be sick of sickness,[133]
And you will then not be sick.[134]
The sage is not sick.
This is because he is sick of sickness.[135]
Therefore, he is not sick.

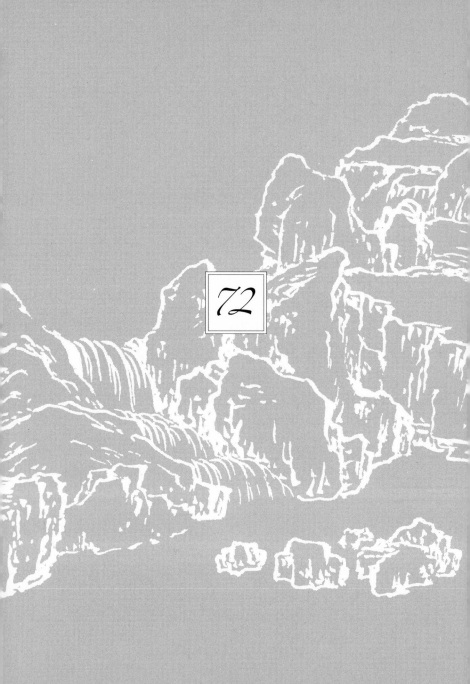

When the people do not respect authority,
     as they might a demon holding a rod,
Then a greater authority will soon arrive reminiscent of
     the days when women ruled the household.

The people should not make light of where they dwell;
Nor should they feel their lives restricted.
Listen, if they don't feel their lives to be restricted,
They will not be restricted.

Therefore the sage
    Knows himself well, but does not display himself;
    Loves himself, but does not make much of himself.
Thus, in each case he takes firm hold of the first and avoids
     the last.

73

He who eagerly takes his courage into his own hands,
  will have his life cut off.
He who restrains his eagerness,
  will have life like gushing water.
Of these two things,
One prepares the ground for cultivation,
  the other suffocates life itself.

Therefore the sage is heavily suspicious and
  considers this difficult.

The Way of heaven
Does not contend, but is good at summoning
  its strength and standing its ground;
It does not speak, but is good at taking what is said to
  heart, and hitting the mark in response.
It does not wave you over to visit,
  but comes of its own accord.
It is loose and easy, but mulls things over well in silence.
Heaven's net is wonderfully vast and enveloping;
Though wide-meshed, nothing slips through.[136]

74

If the people have no fear of death,
    as they might of armed demons,
Why should their eyes open wide with
    fear when death is used as a threat?
Even if the people were constantly afraid of death,
And there were deviant characters
    to be shackled and killed,
Who would be eager to do this?
It is an unchanging fact that there is an official
    executioner[137] at hand in charge of killing.

Listen, killing in place of the official executioner
Is like cutting and planing wood
    in place of a master carpenter.
So take care: he is a rare man who cuts and planes
    in place of a master carpenter,
And does not injure his own hand.

The people starve: there's famine and grains do not ripen.
This is because those above them
        feed excessively on those grains that are taxed.
For this reason, the people starve and face famine.
The people are difficult to manage:
This is because those
        above them are "doers" and fabricators.
For this reason the people are difficult to manage.
The people consider death
        no heavier than pulling a cart empty of baggage.
This is because they seek out life
        as though piling items one atop another.
For this reason they consider death
        no heavier than pulling an empty cart.

Listen, only the man
        who does not do things with "life" in mind,
Will have abundant respect for life itself.

76

Man at birth is soft and flexible;
At death, he is rigid and as hard as clay.
While living, the Ten Thousand Things, especially
    the grasses and trees, are pliant and delicate;
In death, they are withered and desiccated like the
    branches atop an old tree.

Thus, the hard and rigid are the followers of death;
The pliant and flexible are the followers of life.
For this reason, if weapons are too rigid, they will not last.
If trees are too rigid,
    they will be cut down and used as furnishings.[138]
The rigid and large reside below;
The pliant and flexible reside above.

137

77

I suppose heaven's Way is much like drawing a bow:

The upper part is pulled down,

The lower part is pulled up.

Whatever is excessive, it decreases;

Whatever is insufficient, it supplements

      as you might mend a robe with a cloth.

The Way of heaven decreases what is excessive, and

      supplements the insufficient.

The Way of man is not so.

It decreases what is insufficient, and hands it over to the

      already excessive.

Who is capable of having excess and

      handing it over to all under heaven?

Only he who has the Way at hand.

For this reason, the sage

    Acts but relies on nothing;

    Gets his work done, but then moves on.

    He has no desire to show off his personal gifts.

78

There is nothing under heaven as soft and pliant as water;
Yet in striking against the hard and rigid,
There is nothing more capable of success.
This being as it is,
      there is nothing that could easily take its place.

The pliant defeats the rigid;
The soft defeats the hard.
Under heaven, there is no one who does not know this,
But also no one capable of taking this rule step by step.

For this reason, the sage says,
   "Accepting responsibility for the state's blemishes:
   This is called being the main pillar
      of the shrine to the gods of the land.
   Accepting responsibility for the state's ill omens:
   This is called being king of all under heaven."

Unbiased words would appear to be their opposite.

79

In pacifying great rancor,

There will invariably be backbiting that remains.

What good can be made of this?[139]

For this reason, the sage

    Grasps the left side of the contract,[140]

    But does not importune others.

Those with virtue go by the rules of the contract;

Those without virtue go by what they can get away with.

The Way of heaven does not engage in nepotism,

But is unchangingly at the side of the good man.

80

A small state with few people:
Though they have many convenient implements at hand,
  do not have them put into use.
Let the people treat death as weighty, and do not have
  them travel distant roads to settle elsewhere.
 Though they have boats and drawn carriages,
  There will be no occasion to ride in them.
 Though armor and weapons be at hand,
  There will be no occasion to set them out in martial
  display.

Have the people return to the custom of knotting cords
  and putting them to use.[141]
Let them find their food tasty.
Let them find their clothing attractive.
Let them find their homes peaceful.
Let them take pleasure in their long-continued customs.

In this way, neighboring provinces may be
  within sight of each other,
But while the cries of the roosters and
  dogs of one may be heard in the other,
The people will reach old age and turn to dust
And never travel back and forth.

81

Reliable words are not attractive;
Attractive words[142] are not reliable.
Good people do not quibble;
Quibblers are not good people.
The knowing are not know-it-alls;
Know-it-alls are not knowing.[143]

The sage does not hoard:[144]
As much as he does for the sake of others,
He himself has all the more at hand.
The Way of heaven
Clears the ground for cultivation and does not hinder.
The Way of the sage
Is to act but not contend.

FURTHER
EXPLORATIONS

TAOISM AND ZEN

Taoism's Path

A basic tenet of the ideas derived from the old man's book is that all is change, that the field of existence and nonexistence and everything on it is in constant motion and flux. It stands to reason, then, that the philosophy set out by the old man and by his apostles Chuang Tzu and Lieh Tzu could not escape from this law. Indeed, Taoism—the term we generally associate with the teachings of these three men—was only briefly identified solely with them, and eventually established a canon of over a thousand volumes; and Lao Tzu—the name or title generally accepted as the old man's—was soon to be revered and claimed as founder or guiding deity of cults involved in activities as diverse as alchemy, health exercises, collective sexual practices, expeditions out to sea in search of the "Taoist" paradise, and finding a way to eternal life.

How did this happen?

Part of the confusion may have devolved from the term "Tao," or way, itself. For the old man, it meant something completely beyond definition or explanation: a Way that had to be followed—if that word may be used—spontaneously and without previously acquired intellectual baggage. Most importantly, it could not be "grasped" without being distorted. For Chung-ni and the scholars, however, the Way had been well established by the ancient sages and could often be found explained in the classics of antiquity. Thus, it could be acquired by study. The latter "Taoists," it seems, preferred this second definition.

The matter is then further complicated by developments intertwined with Chinese medicine, the study of which dated to far antiquity, surely preceding the early first millennium BCE work, *The Yellow Emperor's Classic on Medicine* (*Huang Ti Nei Ching Su Wen*).

In the third or fourth century BCE, a class of practitioners arose called *fang shih*. This term is variously translated as "recipe masters," "prescription masters," or "magicians," which likely indicates the breadth of their interests. Inheriting over a thousand years of experiments in diet and herbal medicines, these men either worked alone or established schools advocating various practices such as breathing and stretching exercises; strict diets often centered on the avoidance of grains; sexual practices promoting the preservation of vital essences, which were sometimes practiced in group orgies; and alchemical elixirs compounded of cinnabar, lead, gold, and mercury. All were said to lead the participant to longevity, or even immortality.

Such masters and schools quoted—and required their believers to recite—the old man's book, and eventually deified both the Yellow Emperor and the old man as a single supreme god, Huang-Lao. As might be suspected, their interpretations of the old man's book were highly imaginative. For example, one commentary that plays on the opening lines runs as follows:

> "The Tao that can be Tao'd [explained]," this is to eat good things in the morning; "is not the eternal Tao," this is to have a bowel movement in the evening.[1]

Another development in the expanded meaning of "Taoism" was the second century CE establishment of political cults and theocratic states that considered the old man's book a sacred text. Their leaders assumed the title *t'ien shih*, or Heavenly Masters, and, like the *fang shih*, interpreted the book to their own purposes. The most political of the groups were suppressed by the government by the beginning of the third century, but even after that, a number of their sects continued to prosper, led by men who called themselves *tao shih*, or "Masters of the Way."

Add to this that around the third century CE, various men—both as individuals and as groups—developed what has been called the "Pure Conversation School." These men devoted themselves to poetry, music, and the beauty of nature, and wrote in styles reminiscent of the *Tao Te Ching*, the *Chuang Tzu*, and the *Lieh Tzu*. The most famous of these groups—the Seven Sages of the Bamboo Grove—also devoted themselves to wine, unconventional behavior, and an uncompromising spontaneity. When the conversations became so pure that they could go no farther, there was still plenty of wine, which they considered a vehicle to the Tao. Liu Ling (221–300), who always enjoyed a drink, was exemplary:

> Liu Ling is also a person who liked to go about his house naked. Once he was interrupted by some stuffy Confucian visitors. They expressed surprise at the absence of trousers. Liu replied, "The whole universe is my house and this room is my trousers. What are you doing here inside my trousers?"[2]

Finally,[3] there were the sea expeditions sent out from the east coast of China to find the Isles of the Blest. Such expeditions were based on casual references to P'eng-lai, a place where no one grew old or died, in the *Chuang Tzu* and *Lieh Tzu*, and were sponsored by gullible nobility and even an emperor. The leader of one of these expeditions was able to convince its sponsor that he would need to bring along three thousand young men and three thousand young women to prepare a colony for him, and not surprisingly, never returned. But these journeys, too, were included under the large tent of "Taoism," a term now grown so unwieldy that by the fifth century CE it lacked any clear definition at all.

Nevertheless, the old man had pointed out nearly a thousand years before that all things appear, develop, and change, but eventually "each returns to its root" (verse 16). That "return" was now on its way from India in the physical form of a man in his late sixties, a Buddhist eccentric by the name of Bodhidharma.

The First Patriarch

It took Bodhidharma some three years under sail from India to arrive at the Chinese port of Nan-hai in 520 CE.[4] During that time he would have devoted himself, at least in part, to the study of the Chinese language—no doubt talking with the Chinese sailors aboard, but also reading through some of the Chinese classics, one of which would likely have been the old man's text. From Nan-hai, he set out for Lo-yang, and eventually attracted enough attention to be summoned to the Liang-dynasty court of the emperor Wu. This monarch was a devout Buddhist who had spent a good deal of his capital on building temples, having the sutras copied, and supporting monks and nuns. He was astonished, therefore, when he asked Bodhidharma how much merit he would accrue from such activities, and the latter replied, "None at all," explaining that such works were worldly rather than spiritual. Soldiering on, the emperor then asked what the first principle of Buddhism might be, and Bodhidharma gave his now famous reply:

Vast emptiness, nothing holy.

When the exasperated emperor finally asked, "Then who are you?" Bodhidharma responded, "I don't know," and the interview was over.

If not in the lyrical Chinese of the old man, this is the language of a distrust of words, and echoes "the Tao that can be articulately understood is not the Unchanging Way," from a slightly different tack.

Bodhidharma went on to sit in meditation for nine years in a cave that would become the site of the Shaolin temple, to establish himself as the first patriarch of Zen Buddhism in China, to have the first tea plants grow from his eyelids after he cut them off in disgust upon falling asleep during meditation, and to live, it was said, to the rather ripe old age of one hundred and fifty. When he finally died, he was buried at Hsiung-erh Feng,[5] or Bear's Ear Peak, bringing to full circle a connection with the shamans who worshipped the bear in the old man's home kingdom of Ch'u. And like the spirit power of the shaman's bear, Bodhidharma, too, may have been too tough to keep down. Not long after his decease, he was met in the mountains of Turkistan by a Chinese pilgrim returning from India. Wearing only one sandal, as might one of the Sages of the Bamboo Grove, he explained to the pilgrim that he was on his way home to India. When the pilgrim was once back in China, he revealed this event to Bodhidharma's disciples. Opening up the grave, they found it empty but for a single sandal.

Bodhidharma is interesting to us not only for his eccentric behavior and semi-cryptic remarks, but also for two sets of statements he allegedly set down as the very basis of Zen. Both sets resonate with the very pith of the old man's book.

The first is the so-called Four Statements of the Zen Sect, which are as follows:

1. No standing on texts or words[6]
2. A transmission beyond teaching
3. Direct pointing to the mind of man
4. Seeing one's nature and becoming a Buddha

This set of premises neatly parallels some of the basic premises of the old man's philosophy, whether expressed directly or implied. Chung-ni and the scholars worked from and revered the ancient classics, regarding them as essential vehicles for grasping the Tao. The old man, however, had dismissed them with the remark that the authors of such works were now nothing more than dust and dried bones, and he quoted neither ancient sages nor the classics in his work. As for any teaching (including his own, we must assume), he clearly stated that "Those who know, don't speak; those who speak, don't know." The sage concerns himself with filling the people's stomachs rather than their minds, thus keeping "wise men" at bay. He himself fabricates nothing, and conducts himself only according to wordless teachings.

In this connection, the true wise man will throw any and all conceptual baggage overboard, and will not be duped by any such relative notions as good and bad, long and short, or even birth and death.[7] He sees reality without the gauge of judgmental thought or the blinders of desire, and moves with the flow of things, finding nothing to hinder him.

Finally, the man of vision sees his own character, or, in Taoist terms, his fundamental virtue (*te*), and becomes—not a Buddha, in the language of Bodhidharma—but a sage at one with the Tao. Being in accord with his fundamental virtue, he has no consciousness of virtue, and so acts with spontaneity and harmony with all other beings.

The second set of statements or premises, the Meditation on the Four Behaviors, also finds its counterpart in the old man's views:

1. The requital of malice
2. Following one's karma or circumstances
3. Seeking nothing
4. Acting according to the Way

Again, the old man encourages us over and over not to contend, nor to put ourselves above others, but rather to be like water and seek the lowest places. We are encouraged to repress all anger and to nurture love. Conflict, contention, and malice are obstacles to harmony. The old man says,

> Listen, with nurturing love,
> If you are brought into conflict,
>   you will overcome the opposition.
> If you maintain this love, you will be firm.
> When heaven is going to intervene,
> It protects you unexpectedly with nurturing love.   VERSE 67

In the same manner, if we follow our karmic situation or circumstances, we will not contend. This is the natural consequence of acting without acting—without fabrication or fuss. If we harbor resentment or desire, our vision is made unclear, our actions become planned and self-conscious, and in the end we see—not reality—but our own mental projections. Follow circumstances,[8] and you will swim through the raging torrent as though it were a slow-moving stream.[9]

Seeking nothing (or Nothing) is, in Buddhism, seeking the Void; in Taoism, that place where we acquire less and less each day until we can act by "relying on nothing." Again, the less mental baggage, the better. The Zen adept struggles with a koan, and has his responses pummeled by the master until he—the adept—has nothing left to rely on. He must eventually answer with the same spontaneity and nonfabrication the old man encourages us to, and find that suddenly, he is free.

In the end, whether Zen Buddhist or Taoist, one must act in accordance with the Tao. Although Bodhidharma's term is 法, in the Buddhist Law or Dharma, the two terms—*Law* 法 and *Tao* 道—have been used interchangeably by Zen Buddhists from the very beginning. Thus, it is not by accident that the answer to one of the most important questions in Zen—What is the meaning of Bodhidharma's coming from the West? (i.e., What is the true essence of Buddhism?)—is answered with the definitive phrase:

> To travel the Tao, this is the meaning of
> Bodhidharma's coming from the West.

Seng-ts'an and the Hsin Hsin Ming—*Taoist Zen or Zen Taoism?*

It is often said that Zen is really Taoism in Buddhist robes.[10] The main argument for this statement is that Buddhism, as it came from the great Buddhist universities in India, was much too metaphysical and cerebral for the Chinese, whose appetite was really more inclined toward the lyrical thought of the old man, and the fancifulness of Chuang Tzu and Lieh Tzu (and, we might add, the practicality of Chung-ni and his scholars). Thus, even though there were strong similarities between the Emptiness of Indian Buddhist *sunyata* and the Nothingness of Taoist *wu*, the intellectual flights of the Indian religion would have to be brought down to the Chinese Earth. Bodhidharma had planted the seed of this Sinification with his stripped-down meditative brand of Buddhism, but the real integration of Buddhism and Taoism would be achieved by Seng-ts'an, the Third Patriarch of Zen, in his short poetic work, the *Hsin Hsin Ming* (*An Inscription on Faith in the Mind*).

Seng-ts'an (d. 606) was a native Chinese about whom little is known. The bare-bone facts seem to be that he lived during a time of Buddhist persecution, and had to feign losing his mind in order to avoid losing his head, wandering some fifteen years in a state of homelessness. It is said that he *was* at home with wild tigers—the Chinese symbol for the Earth—thus demonstrating that he was truly grounded and without obstruction.[11]

The *Hsin Hsin Ming* is one of the earliest Chinese-authored writings on Zen, and the old man's influence on it is apparent from its famous first line:

> The ultimate Tao is not difficult,
> Just be unwilling to pick and choose.

Although this verse echoes the early Buddhist Third Noble Truth—that attachment, to both phenomena and noumena, is the cause of all suffering—and hints at the Mahayana Buddhist teaching of nonduality, the vocabulary and phrasing are pure Taoist. Right from the beginning, Seng-ts'an uses the word "Tao" rather than the Buddhist term *Dharma*, and assures the reader that this Way "is not difficult," rather than somberly informing him or her that this may take many incarnations of hard and serious work. Just do not be disposed to "picking and choosing," a term that can also mean "discrimination." This has more an atmosphere of "free and easy wandering" than Bodhidharma's sitting in meditation for nine years facing a wall. And as we read through the *Hsin Hsin Ming*, we find that there is much more of the old man's letting things alone than the dour Buddhist paradigm of rules and regulations for almost every human activity.

The following are other verses from this Chinese cornerstone of Zen Buddhism that may illustrate the Taoist undercurrent that runs through Zen even today.

> Simply neither hate nor love;
> It will be clear without a doubt.
>
> If you would like to grasp its appearance,
> Don't reside in "right" or "wrong."
>
> Being unaware of the mysterious purport of things,
> You will uselessly belabor your peace of mind.
>
> Perfect within itself, a Great Void—
> There is nothing lacking, nothing superfluous.
>
> With much talk and much thought,
> You tumble and turn, and nothing is right.
>
> Cut off speech, cut off thought
> There's no place you cannot penetrate.
>
> There's no need to search for the truth;
> Just give your opinions a rest.

Let things go, and they'll be spontaneous and natural;
Get to the essence, and there's no going or staying.

Entrust things to your nature, and you'll be in accord with
  the Tao;
Wander free and easy, and you'll cut off distress.

The sage fabricates nothing;
The fool fetters himself.

Gain and loss, right and wrong:
Let them all go right away.

When all phenomena are contemplated equally,
They return to the natural and spontaneous.

Beyond all words and speech;
There is no past, present, or future.

By the time of Zen Buddhism's arrival in China in the sixth century, Chinese culture had been permeated by the contents of the old
man's book for over a thousand years. It is not surprising, therefore,
that Zen—sharing a number of similar tenets of Taoism from the
very beginning—would have absorbed a good bit of Taoism's charac-
teristics and flavor. This is evident in the vocabulary of Zen writings
like the *Hsin Hsin Ming* and many others. The Taoist sense of humor,
so well illustrated in the works of Chuang Tzu and Lieh Tzu, as well
as the irreverence of the Seven Sages of the Bamboo Grove, reappear
in the stories of the Zen patriarchs and their koans.[12]

In the arts, this absorption of Taoist traits by Zen can also be
seen in a genre of Chinese landscape painting in which the painter

is encouraged to plumb the nature of his subject and to understand its flow of *ch'i*.[13] And although the vocabulary here is Taoist or from the more mystical branch of Confucianism, and although the Zen painter might declare that the painter and the subject (and the brush and paper) must become one, the intent is the same. Is the painting Taoist inspired or informed by Zen? The answer may not be so clear. The same question might be put, with similar results, to certain styles of Chinese poetry.[14]

It could be argued that such absorption may have been necessary for the survival of a foreign religion in a socially conservative society, but this is probably not the case. As Chung-ni might have said,[15] there is a single spiritual thread that runs through the old man, Bodhidharma, and Seng-ts'an. That thread, however, is not so directly grasped, for,

> You may look for it, but it cannot be seen;
> You may listen for it, but it may not be heard.
>
> —*Zenrin Kushu*, *Chung Yung*, and others

Better we should not make too much of a fuss of it, but simply avoid picking and choosing.

THE *TAO TE CHING* AND THE MARTIAL ARTS

Both the old man and the young Chung-ni would have come from the class of scholars, and so presumably would have been predisposed to civilian rather than military rule. But both were also educated men and understood that ever since the establishment of the Chou dynasty in the twelfth century BCE, the paradigm in China had been one of the balance of the cultural and the martial. In this way, the ideal man was the "gentleman" who studied both the arts of peace and the arts of war, and was thus prepared for any eventuality.

Although Chung-ni seemed to have had a distaste for military tactics in general,[1] he understood the necessity of armies and officers, and admired courage on the field, especially if it was accompanied by self-effacement.[2] And it must be remembered that when his disciple was asked where Chung-ni got his education, he replied, "The Way of *Wen* and *Wu*," or the Way of the cultural and the martial.[3] Although this phrase may have been a reference to Chung-ni's interest in the martial arts, especially archery, that cannot be confirmed.

The old man, however, was more outspoken, and two of his verses in the *Tao Te Ching* have been taken as statements of his outright pacifism:

He who would wholeheartedly help
    the ruler of men by means of the Way
Will not use military weapons
    to force himself on the world.
In putting his hands to things,
    he prefers returning to the fundamental Way.
Wherever troops bivouac,
    thorny shrubs and spiny brambles grow.
After the clashes of great armies,
    years of empty fields and open mouths
    will inevitably be at hand.   VERSE 30

Listen, well-polished weapons are inauspicious tools;
All creatures consistently back away from them.
Thus, a man who possesses the Way
    will not have them around. . . .

[W]eapons are inauspicious tools,
And they are not the tools of the Gentleman.
He uses them only when it can't be helped,
And considers tranquility and simplicity
    to be the highest good.
Victory he does not find beautiful,
For to do so would be to enjoy killing others.
And listen, the man who enjoys killing others
Will find his ambitions thwarted in this world.   VERSE 31

But many passages of his work seem to be outright words of advice to military men, and so invite at least a passing comparison with a book on warfare written by his contemporary Sun Tzu, and to comments derived from the old man's work but filtered through the vocabulary of Zen on individual combat. The book on warfare, entitled the *Sun Tzu* after its author, or *The Art of War*, is one of the most highly respected manuals on warfare in the history of mankind. The comments on individual combat range from men as disparate as Zen monks, who on taking Buddhist orders had pledged to save mankind, and swordsmen who fought with very real weapons.

The Tao Te Ching *and* The Art of War

> *Things are complex, but one does not worry about their being chaotic; they change, but one does not worry about their being confused.* —Wang Pi[4]

To grasp the nexus between the *Tao Te Ching* and *The Art of War*, we must again take a step back—in this case about six hundred years—to the *I Ching*, a book dealing with the almost primordial Chinese understanding of the transformation of the world through the modalities of yin and yang.

Fundamental to this understanding is that yin and yang, in all of their many manifestations, are not only in opposition to each other, but are also forces that are mutually defining, substantiating, nurturing, and limiting. Most importantly, their expressions in phenomena—from meteorological changes, to terrestrial conditions, to the situations in which man finds himself—are not haphazard, but are regulated and integrated by a controlling principle inherent in them all: the Tao. This principle is manifested in patterns followed by everything in the universe and that are symbolized by the sixty-four hexagrams of the *I Ching*.

The good news is that these patterns can be understood. Chungni, who made a study of the *I Ching*, wrote:

In Heaven they take form as phenomena, on Earth as shapes; thus, transformation and change can be seen.

Chung-ni further noted in his commentary that as the book takes the measure of Heaven and Earth, we are able not only to see, but actually to grasp the broad warp and woof of their Tao. Through the study of the *I Ching*, he said, we may come to resemble Heaven and Earth and thus not set ourselves against them. In this way, our knowledge is in rhythm with the Ten Thousand Things, the Tao (through us) brings order to all under Heaven, and we make no mistakes. The man or men who compiled the *I Ching* contemplated these patterns, understood how they converged and became interrelated, and set down the symbols, judgments, and images of their unchanging paths. Finally, Chung-ni noted that

When you completely grasp the mysterious and understand transformation, your virtue[5] will be overflowing.

It is not difficult to imagine that such a study would be of interest both to a man whose philosophy was to live his life without conflict and to one whose very profession was conflict and its speedy resolution.

No doubt the old man and Sun Tzu were profoundly influenced by the *I Ching*, which was already an ancient classic by the sixth century BCE; and no doubt both read into it and took from it according to their own predilections. Sun Tzu, for example, may have pondered a long time over the very first hexagram *Ch'ien* (乾), often translated as the Creative, but associated with power, continual energy, action, and light, and the image of heaven, the sun, and the leaders of men. While the reading of the six lines of the hexagram can be complex and more instructive to the initiated, several passages under its heading may indicate—even to the layman—why it would have been of interest to any actively engaged military man:

> The leader's head appears above the mass of beings, and ten thousand countries are united peacefully.

> Heaven moves robustly. The Gentleman is of himself strong, and does not rest.

> The Way of the Creative transforms and changes; each thing thus becomes correct in nature, protects and engages with great harmony.

> The Gentleman is actively creative the entire day.

> The arrogant dragon leader will have regrets.

The old man, on the other hand, whose most famous byword was to "act without acting," would have been more attracted to the second hexagram *K'un* (坤), the Receptive: the Earth, the dark, the female, and the yielding. Recall that, for the old man, the sage "resides in nonfabrication," and that "the gate of the dark and mysterious female is called the root of Heaven and Earth." Under the Receptive, the old man would have found directives, not for the military man, but for the retiring sage:

> Taking the lead, you become confused and lose the Way.
> Bringing up the rear in the order of things, you receive the unchanging.

Leading, you will become lost;
Going behind, you receive mastery.

Far-reaching, indeed, is being founded in the Receptive;
The Ten Thousand Things are born because of it.

He does not practice,
But nothing is without preparation for development.

The Way of the Receptive is in order;
It acknowledges heaven's [will] and acts in [proper] time.

Nevertheless, there is a unifying link between *Ch'ien* and *K'un*, and that is the *I Ching*'s principle of transformation. This was discussed in broad terms by the old man, but strictly in terms of warfare by Sun Tzu, and it is interesting that the old man, who understood the world through the concept of nonexistence, rarely mentions "transformation" as such, although it is the undercurrent of his entire work. Sun Tzu, on the other hand, dealt with the active world of existence, and refers to transformation repeatedly. For both, it was the ever-changing foundation upon which they both stood with ease.[6]

With this as a background, we may look at several passages from the *Tao Te Ching* and *The Art of War* to see how they deal with certain concepts informed by the paradigm of flow.

Tao Te Ching = ◎
The Art of War = ◈

◎ There is nothing under Heaven as soft and pliant as water;
Yet in striking against the hard and rigid,

There is nothing more capable of success.   VERSE 78

○ The pliant defeats the rigid.   VERSE 78

◇ Military tactics are like water in form and shape.
Water in its flow avoids the high and hurries to the low.   XI, 29

◇ The speed of rushing water has a force that will roll away
stones.   V, 12

○ The Way drifts buoyantly, now left, now right.   VERSE 34

◇ Thus, do not repeat [a military tactic that gave you] one victory;
Respond to form, and [your tactics] will be unlimited.   VI, 28

◇ Thus, as water has no constant shape, tactics have no constant
course.   VI, 32

○ The sage does not have an unchanging mind.   VERSE 49

◇ Therefore,
The general who has penetrated the benefit of various transformations will understand how to use tactics.   VIII, 4

○ For movement, the right timing is considered good.   VERSE 8

◇ For this reason,
The good warrior ... does not lose [the moment] for
defeating the enemy.   IV, 14

From these few examples we might imagine that the man of the
Tao, be he a scholar-bureaucrat as was the old man, or a military
commander like Sun Tzu,[7] understood that life is constant change
and transformation, while its opposite, death, is stasis. The old man
notes that "Man at birth is soft and flexible; at death, he is rigid and
hard as clay" (verse 76), while Sun Tzu declares outright that his art
is one of "managing transformation" (VII, 32). Thus, both men saw

the virtue of traveling the grid of existence, bending with the changes in circumstances, and staying pliant and forever aware of transformation.

Tradition considers the writers of these two books to have been contemporaries of the sixth century BCE, although recent scholarship has cast doubts on the true dates of both. Furthermore, there is nothing in the literature of the period indicating that either man was influenced by or was even aware of the existence of the other. Yet there are common points in the two books that arrest our attention even at a glance. The likely truth is that the standard raised by the Chou more than half a millennium before them—that the true Way is the Tao of the Cultural and the Military—permeated the thoughts of both men, and that the principles of the *I Ching* were so deep-seated in their consciousnesses that these common points appeared naturally, rather than by design.

The following are further selections from the two works that might substantiate a common cognizance if not a common source:

◉ Use the military in an unexpected manner.   VERSE 57
◈ Attack where he is unprepared;
　Appear where he does not expect you.   I, 24

◉ Act without fabrication.
　　Do the job without putting your hand to it.   VERSE 63
◈ Therefore, the skillful tactician defeats the opponent's troops
　　without fighting.   III, 6

◆ For this reason, having a hundred victories in a hundred battles
   is not the greatest good.
The greatest good is in defeating the opponent without
   fighting.   III, 2

◉ There is a saying for the use of weapons:
   Do not be eager to act as the host; rather, act as the guest.
   Do not be eager to advance an inch; rather, step back a foot.
This is said to be moving forward without doing so;
Striking and retreating without extending your elbow;
Seizing your opponent without a weapon,
And taking over while having no opponent at all.   VERSE 69

◆ For this reason, the victorious strategist first wins
   and then seeks to fight.
The losing strategist first fights and then seeks to win.   IV, 15

◉ There is no greater disaster than making light of your opponent;
Making light of your opponent almost always results
   in losing your treasures as easily as leaves fall
   from the trees.   VERSE 69

◆ Listen, when you do not really think ahead,
And consider your enemy an easy one,
   you are going to be taken captive.   IX, 41

◉ Thus, when opponents meet with raised weapons,
The one who laments the fight will win.   VERSE 69

◆ Leaders should not advance their troops out of anger;
Generals should not go into battle out of hotheadedness.   XII, 18

◉ He who knows others may have knowledge
   enough to predict the rain,

But he who knows himself
>> will see with the clarity of the sun and moon.
He who is victorious over others has strength,
But he who is victorious over himself
>> will have the potency of a swarm of bees.   VERSE 33

◇ Thus, the saying:
>> If you know the opponent and know yourself, you may
>> fight a hundred battles and not stand on shaky ground.
>> If you do not know the opponent, but know yourself, you
>> will have one victory for every loss.
>> If you do not know the opponent or yourself, you will be
>> on shaky ground every time you fight.   III, 18

The Tao and the Martial Arts of Japan

The Sword and Zen are of the same essence.

—Yagyu Munenori

The old man's work was probably first introduced to Japan in the sixth or seventh century CE. Chinese literature was being imported at that time for the purpose of making Japan more culturally cosmopolitan, better versed in the philosophy and structure of government, and, in the process, more literate. The bulk of the books being brought in were the standards of the Confucian canon, which by this time included the *I Ching*. But other classics were also taught, and the old man's book would undoubtedly have been one of them.[8] While the work itself likely became the hereditary study of one of the aristocratic clans assigned to specialize in Chinese subjects, in due time it was studied, either in its original form or through the filter of Zen Buddhism, by another group of specialists: the warrior class.

The beginning of the association of the old man's book with Japanese swordsmanship is unclear. In the twelfth century, the legendary swordsman Kiichi Hogen, who is said to have lived near a canal in the ancient capital of Kyoto, left equivocal statements like the following:

If the opponent comes, then greet him; if he goes, then send him off. To five add five and make ten; to two add eight and make ten. By this you create harmony. Judge the situation, know the mind. The great is ten feet square, the small enters the tiniest speck. The action may be fierce, but when facing what is in front of you, don't move the mind.

This sounds like a mixture of *I Ching* numerology, yin/yang philosophy, and the *Tao Te Ching*, and it is interesting to note that Hogen supposedly taught his style only to "the Eight Priests of Kurama."[9] By the sixteenth century, however, we find the old man's work being quoted or paraphrased by some of the greatest swordsmen of all times, who were often well-educated in the classics and deeply steeped in the ideal of the cultured warrior. The following are a few of the key concepts of the *Tao Te Ching* that may have found resonance in the minds of these men as they contemplated the deeper aspects of their art.

The Way that can be articulately described
      is not the Unchanging Way.
The name that can be said out loud
      is not the Unchanging Name.   VERSE I

This is the keynote of the old man's book, and the foundation of his thought. It reminds us that words, definitions, and verbal concepts are all human constructs, and therefore tenuous. They are only the packaging that conceals the true content of the world, which is not to be taken for the Real Thing. In the early Zen Buddhist work, the *Hsin Hsin Ming*, this is amplified in the statement, "If the mind makes no discriminations, all things are as they really are." Again, try to define something, and you have put it in a box; it no longer has the freedom of its own character, and has, for all practical purposes, lost its *te*.

Both Yagyu Munenori and Miyamoto Musashi, arguably the greatest swordsmen of the late sixteenth and early seventeenth centuries, took this admonition and applied it to their practice. Both wrote of the value of No Mind, the mind freed of binding concepts, and how such a mind provided freedom of action. Although both taught their students stances and strikes as a part of the art, they also warned against being caught by them in actual practice. Munenori considered any attachment to thoughts or concepts as a "sickness" or a fixation. In the *Clan Traditions of the Martial Arts*, he wrote, "In the martial arts, it is a sickness if you do not leave the mind of the martial arts." Similarly, Musashi argued that being attached to ideas or forms meant immobility, and "Immobility means a dead hand."

Takuan, a Zen monk with connections to both Munenori and Musashi, concluded that the mind (and hence the body) should not be detained by thoughts, strategies, or even material objects like swords. He wrote, "In Buddhism, we call this stopping of the mind 'delusion.'" To say this in reverse, that delusion (the Tao that can be defined, the name that can be pronounced) is a stopping of the mind, perhaps clarifies the fatal consequences this would mean to the warrior. Freedom of action, freedom of response, requires freedom from the heavy baggage of calcified conceptual thought.

He acts, but relies on nothing.

This is the most repeated phrase in the old man's book, appearing in verses 2, 10, 51, and 77, and is a corollary to the above. The martial artist must not only *not* rely on his learned ideas while in action, but must also be free to use whatever is at hand during a confrontation. Munenori wrote that the martial artist should toss out all concepts, as they would only get in the way, and Musashi demonstrated this in a very physical way a number of times in his career, once even picking up a stick he was carving as a bow when suddenly confronted by a challenger. His famous duel on Ganryu Island demonstrated clearly what can happen to a man, no matter how talented, who relies on a certain sword or a special technique. In this duel, Musashi defeated the feared swordsman Sasaki Kojiro, who excelled at swordsmanship but relied on an extra-long sword, while Musashi used an impromptu wooden sword carved from an oar. In his own book, *The Book of Five Rings*, Musashi argued against relying upon, or having preferences for, a certain length of sword or a special stance in combat. He wrote that "with weapons, just as with other things, you should not make distinctions or preferences."

One should move without restraint with the circumstances, entirely—as Chuang Tzu put it—as "free and easy wandering." Indeed, the very beginning words of the *Hsin Hsin Ming* note that "The Tao is not difficult; just avoid picking and choosing." Preconceptions and prejudices, mental or physical, are to be thrown overboard so that the mind can move on its unchartered course downstream:

The Great Way drifts buoyantly; now left, now right.

The old man wrote that the greatest good is like water, which constantly flows and "contends with none." The Zen monk Takuan noted in his letter to Munenori that "the mind of the man who has arrived does not stop at one thing for even a bit. It is like pushing down a gourd in the water." And, "it is like a ball riding a swift-moving current; [in Zen] we respect the mind that flows on like this and does not stop for an instant in any place." The martial artist, too, must flow like water, and not be detained by anything.[10] In *The Book of Five Rings*, Musashi dedicated an entire chapter to this element, and emphasized fluidity as being all-important. He wrote that "the heart of [his] martial art of the Two Heavens Style takes water as its foundation," and that "one makes the mind like water." Like Takuan, he meant that this water should be, not placid, but a moving stream, and added that one should "not let the mind stand still even when you are in repose." His statement that one should "strike with all the power of momentarily restrained water bursting forth from a stream" is underscored by the old man's "There is nothing under heaven as soft and pliant as water; yet in striking against the hard and the rigid, there is nothing more capable of success" (verse 78).

Ito Ittosai, another master of swordsmanship roughly contemporary with Munenori and Musashi, took this image of water and applied it in yet a different way. He stated to his students that "the ten thousand transformations all turn from the One. The One is the complete body of the formless. It is, for example, like water. Water has no unchanging form; thus it is able to follow the square or round shape of the pot [into which it is put]." Whether termed Mind or No Mind, this One is the source of all techniques, moves, and strategies, which will flow from it like water if it is not impeded by words, thoughts, or previously learned concepts.[11]

Understanding the Unchanging is called the bright and clear.
If you do not understand the Unchanging,
You will be doing things in the dark,
    and this is ill-omened.   VERSE 16

The old man used the term *ch'ang*, the Unchanging, to under-
score many of the key concepts of his work—the Unchanging Tao,
the Unchanging Name, the Unchanging Virtue, or *Te*—and it
should be understood that the term itself is central to his understanding of the Great Way.

Originally, the term meant "long," as in a long bolt of cloth,
and later, by extension, "unchanging" or "constant." In modern
Chinese, *ch'ang ch'uan* means a river flowing without interrup-
tion, and this may be a helpful image to keep in mind. In the text,
the old man says,

Returning to its root is called tranquility,
And this is called returning to its naturally given course.
Returning to its naturally given course is
    called the Unchanging.   VERSE 16

Thus, the Unchanging is not static or calcified; rather, it constantly
and tranquilly flows according to its own nature.

This essential term was quickly adopted by the Zen Buddhists,
who used it to describe the original state of Mind, the mind beyond
conceptual thinking and illusion. This they called the *ch'ang hsin*,
which in Zen literature is most often translated as the "everyday
mind," or the "ordinary mind." One of the most famous and eluci-
dating examples of its use is found in the nineteenth case of the
Wumen Kuan (Japanese: *Mumon Kan*), the thirteenth-century

Chinese collection of Zen koans. The case is important enough in the thought of Zen and swordsmanship to be quoted fully:

> Nan-ch'uan was asked by Chao-chou, "What is the Tao?" Nan-ch'uan said, "Your ordinary mind is the Tao." Chao-chou said, "Can you track it down or not?" and Nan-ch'uan replied, "As soon as you look for it, it departs." Chao-chou then asked, "If you can't look for it, how will you know that it's the Tao?" Nan-ch'uan said, "The Tao is not bound to knowing or not knowing. Knowing is confusion; not knowing is being blindsided. If you truly arrived at the Tao of no doubt, it is like a great void or vast vacuity. How can you force this into confirmation or negation?"

The phrase is also quoted in Chapter 28 of the *Ching-te Ch'uan-teng Lu* (Japanese: *Keitoku Dentoroku*), a book compiled in 1004, relating the words and deeds of over six hundred Zen masters:

> The Tao does not use practice. Simply have no blots or stains. How can there be no blots or stains? It is just this: when you have the mind of life and death, when you have the plan of making something, it is all blots and stains. If you want to encounter the Tao directly, the everyday mind is the Tao. What we call the everyday mind fabricates nothing, does not distinguish plus or minus, does not grasp or throw away, finds nothing regular or irregular, and sees no secular or holy.

This is an undercurrent that runs through *The Book of Five Rings*, and Musashi states directly that "In the Way [Tao] of the Martial Arts, do not let your mind be any different from your everyday mind."

But it is in Munenori's *Clan Traditions of the Martial Arts* that it is discussed fully, and in which we feel the resonant connection with the old man's words best:

> The above anecdote [between Nan-ch'uan and Chao-chou] contains a principle that runs through all disciplines. When an explanation of the Way is requested, the answer is "Your ordinary mind." This is truly profound....
>
> Apply this to the world of the arts. When practicing archery, if your mind is occupied by thoughts of shooting the bow, your aim will be inaccurate and wavering. When using a sword, if your mind is occupied with thoughts of plying the sword, its path is unlikely to be stable. When practicing calligraphy, if your mind is occupied by thoughts of writing, the brush will be unsettled. When playing the *koto*, if your mind is filled with thoughts of plucking the strings, the melody will be confused.
>
> When the man shooting the bow forgets about the mind that is shooting the bow and releases the string with the ordinary mind he has when doing nothing, the bow will be tranquil. When plying the sword, riding a horse, writing something, or playing the *koto*, take up the ordinary mind that does none of these or anything at all. Then no matter what you do, you will do it with ease.

The message is clear: let the mind flow on its natural and uninterrupted course, fabricating nothing, and there will be nothing you cannot manage. Or as the old man says or implies throughout the *Tao Te Ching*, act without fabrication.

This is perhaps the end lesson, the summing up, of the old man's work. When we toss away definitions and preconceptions, rely on nothing but our own innate characters, and live within the flow of our unchanging or everyday mind, we then may be able to act without "acting," and be Of-Ourselves-So. To the sword master, this is absolutely paramount. If the practitioner acts otherwise, he will trip over his own self-absorbing consciousness of what he is doing. Acting self-consciously or with a mind preoccupied with techniques and strategies, he will not act freely, and those techniques and strategies will then become an extra sword in the hand of his opponent.

Munenori recommended consistent hard practice until techniques become natural or part of ourselves. This he described as a wedge being used to extract another wedge—using technique in order to eliminate technique. To act, in other words, without fabrication. This is a loosening of attachments, or in the old man's words, nonaccumulation.

Musashi complained in *The Book of Five Rings* about teachers creating complicated techniques—ways of handling the sword, body postures, or hand positions—that only confused the student. This, he said, created attractive flowers, but little fruit. Munenori, with his phrase "The sword and Zen are of the same essence," indicates the same message in that the fundamental meaning of the Chinese character for Zen (禅) is "to manifest (示) the simple (単)." And this, indeed, may have been what the young Chung-ni, a martial artist himself, meant when he said, two thousand years before Munenori and Musashi's time, that "In archery, we do not place major importance on the target."

About one hundred kilometers northeast of Tokyo is the city of Mito, officially founded in the thirteenth century but likely of a much more ancient origin. This was at one time the headquarters of one of the three branches of the Tokugawa family, and the lord of the house of Mito occupied the special position of vice shogun.

Mito Castle eventually became a center of classical Chinese studies, and the samurai of the clan were well known for their traditionalist views.

Within the precincts of the modern city still exists one of the oldest dojos, or martial arts training centers, in the area. Every morning before dawn, in heat or cold, students of all ages arrive to practice kendo, one of the Japanese arts of swordsmanship. The training is intense, and sometimes a younger student still of kindergarten age will cry at the initial strangeness of the surroundings and the armor that he or she will have to don. The master of the dojo, a septuagenarian, will encourage the child with an expression at once firm and tender. The students will likely continue their practice there into adulthood, and what they learn and absorb there will have a lasting influence on their characters.

Not the least of influences will be the atmosphere of the wide and open training room, which is nearly bare of any décor. The floor is constructed of simple stout wooden boards, polished daily by the students themselves. On one wall, reflected vaguely on the dark but shining floor is a single wooden plaque on which is written:

The cultural and the martial are not separate paths.

This expresses an ideal that was formed at the beginning of the Chou dynasty over three thousand years ago, and is manifestly still alive today. The old man understood that ideal, and did not ignore the fact that living in the world often involves strife. The answer to his question, "Who can gradually clarify the muddy water with tranquility?" is still being composed in the dojo at Mito and in a thousand others around the world today.

NOTES

PREFACE

1   Chan, Wing-tsit. *A Source Book in Chinese Philosophy*, p. 137.

2   There are any number of interesting and excellent translations of the *Tao Te Ching*. I would suggest that those readers who would like to do comparative reading in this work would do well by starting with translations by Wing-tsit Chan, John C. Wu, and Red Pine, all of whose works I have admired over the years.

INTRODUCTION

1   This is but one of the traditional dates given for this event. All dates noted in this book are the traditionally accepted ones, and are debated by modern scholars.

2   The two Chous are unrelated.

3   It may be interesting to note in passing that King Wen 文王 is literally Literature (or Culture) King, while his son's name, King Wu 武王, means Warrior King. The Chou dynasty would be held in the deepest respect by the following ages in China and Japan as well, and a balance of *wen* 文 and *wu* 武 would become the paradigm of the fully developed or refined man. This would be expressed by the Chinese character for "beautiful" or "beautiful balance": 斌, *pin* in Chinese, *uruwashii* in Japanese.

    Duke Sun-chao of Wei asked Tzu-kung, "Where did Chung-ni get his education?" Tzu-kung said, "The Way of Wen and Wu (文武之道)."

    —*Analects*, 19:22

4   In ancient times, the character for "king" was interchangeable with the character for "jewel" 玉, indicating the three threads of the necklace holding the jewel. This has been connected to the mystical number three of Northeast Asian shamanism, or possibly to the three souls believed by the people living in that area to inhabit the human body.

5   It should be noted that over time the scholars came from different areas and backgrounds, and naturally had very different temperaments. Thus, they were not all of one mind. It is unlikely, however, that many were so conservative or hyper-orthodox that they would insist on a strict return to the past, and ignore current circumstances. Confucius himself promoted a balanced approach and advocated "warming up the old and knowing the new" (温故而知新).

6   E.g., Kung-fu Tzu, Meng Tzu, Chuang Tzu, Han-fei Tzu, etc.

7   Chan, p. 138.

8   Three quotes from the Confucian *Analects* will illustrate this:
> The Master did not speak about the strange, feats of strength, chaos, or spirits.   —*Analects*, 7:20
> Respect the gods, but keep them at a distance.   —*Analects*, 6:22
> The people in the south have a saying: "A man without constancy could not even be a shaman." That's a good one.   —*Analects*, 13:22

9   Red Pine, p. xiii.

10   Eliade, p. 460.

11   There may be a strong resistance to this way of thinking. We like tidiness in our histories, and may feel a certain uneasiness about authorship when its veracity is questioned. Thus, the ideas that "Homer" may have been any number of Greek storytellers, or that Shakespeare may have had assistant ghostwriters, are not happy ones. In Ssu-ma Ch'ien's description of the old man, he gives him one of the traditional names we know him by, Lao Tan, and even gives the location of the prefecture and village where he was born. Apparently, you can visit (if the Chinese officials will allow it) the place today. But given the distance in time even between "Lao Tan's" life and that of Ssu-ma Ch'ien, and the twenty-five hundred years of earthquakes, devastating wars, and the migrations of whole populations since that time, I would take claims to the old man's birthplace in the same spirit as the signs all over the east coast of America that claimed "George Washington Slept Here" when I was a boy.

12   As a multiple of 3, number 81 is sometimes said to further suggest the shamanic influence on the book. The number 3 is often considered a mystical number by shamans, being both the number of souls that inhabit the body and the number worlds in which we live.

13   Virtue in the sense derived from the word *virtus*, manliness or power. That is, the merit or value of a thing.

14 Although Ch'in Shih Huang Ti, the first real emperor of China, unified, or rather, standardized the written language along with weights, measures, and taxes, he would have been unable to do the same with the spoken language. China is a huge country, divided by a great number of natural barriers, and these conditions have facilitated the development of diverse cultures and diverse dialects. Thus, Cantonese, Mandarin (Pekinese), and Hakka—to name a few of these dialects—are not mutually understood except through the writing system.

15 The term "modern characters" is misleading. The Chinese writing system used today evolved over a number of centuries, and may have first appeared in the form called "Scribe characters," or *Lishu,* sometime between 200 BCE and 200 CE The truly modern *Kaishu* appears about 100 CE And, although Ch'in Shih Huang Ti standardized writing with what are called "Small Seal characters," or *Hsiao chuan*, they were used mostly by the ruling class during the Ch'in dynasty's short reign (221–206 BCE) and for a brief period thereafter. They are now used solely as a form of calligraphic art.

16 This description is, again, very general and somewhat misleading. There are several different subdivisions of Chinese characters, ranging from pure pictographs—both simple and complex—to sketches of ideas, to characters based solely on phonetics, to those consisting of combinations of phonetics and significs.

17 Similarly, during the Cultural Revolution, Mao Tse-tung reasoned that mandarin oranges and other citrus fruits were vestiges of bourgeois society. It naturally followed that he should order all of the citrus crops—citrus, a fruit that had been developed carefully and lovingly in China since ancient times—to be destroyed. A number of farmers and agriculturalists, however, were brave enough to hide enough seedlings to survive the cultural storm, and as a result, the Chinese still have these fruits today.

18 I transmit, but do not create; I stand by those words and love the past.

—*Analects*, 7:1

19 From *Daigaku-chuyo* (*The Great Learning*), Section II, in Shimada Kenji, ed., *Daigaku-chuyo*. Tokyo: Asahi Shimbunsha, 1967.

20 King Wen's son, who is said to have written the text to the *I Ching*.

21 *Analects*, 13:3.

22 Those who speak do not know; those who know are silent.

These words I heard from the old gentleman [Lao Tzu].
If this old gentleman of the Tao really knows,
Why did he himself write five thousand words?

—Po Chu-i (ca. 846 CE)

23 *Analects*, 15:29.

24 *Lieh Tzu*, Chap. 2.

25 See *The Canterbury Tales* by Geoffrey Chaucer:
Whan that Aprill, with his shoures soote
The droghte of March hath perced to the roote
And bathed every veyne in swich licour
Of which *vertu* engendred is the fleur . . .

26 In Chinese, the word *tzu jan* 自然 means both "nature" and "spontaneous."

27 Trying to use words, and every attempt
Is a wholly new start, and a different kind of failure
Because one has only learnt to get the better of words
For the thing one no longer has to say, or the way in which
One is no longer disposed to say it. And so each venture
Is a new beginning, a raid on the inarticulate
With shabby equipment always deteriorating
In the general mess of imprecision of feeling,
Undisciplined squads of emotion.

—T. S. Eliot, "East Coker"

28 Chan, p. 136.

29 *Ibid.*, p. 137.

30 Tu Wei-ming in *Nature in Asian Traditions of Thought*, p. 81.

31 The twentieth-century Japanese philosopher Nishida Kitaro begins his *An Inquiry into the Good* (*Zen no Kenkyu*) with, "Experience means knowing reality just as it is. It is knowing and being in accordance with reality, tossing off all of our own fabrications."   —*Zen no Kenkyu*, p. 13

32 Don't listen to things with your ears. Listen to things with your mind. Don't listen to things with your mind. Listen to them with your *ch'i*. Listening stops in the ears; the mind stops in phenomena.   —*Chuang Tzu*, Chap. 24

33 Tzu Yu suddenly became ill. Tzu Ssu went over to ask after him and said, "This is fantastic! The Creator of Things is about to make something all bent and curved out of you. He's twisted your back into a lump, and your internal organs are now higher than your head. Your chin is hidden in your

navel, your shoulders are up above your head, and your topknot points to the heavens. This must be some tampering with the *ch'i* of yin and yang."

His mind at peace and without any worry, Tzu Yu dragged himself along and looked at his reflection in the well. "Well now," he said. "The Creator of Things is making this bent-up thing out of me."

Tzu Ssu said, "Is this disagreeable to you?"

"Not at all," Tzu Yu said. "Is there any reason for feeling like that? If this condition proceeds on like this, perhaps he'll eventually transform my left elbow into a rooster, and I'll announce the hours of the night. Or, if it goes on in this way, he may transform my right elbow into a crossbow, and I can provide someone with roasted owl. Again, if this continues, he may transform my buttocks into wheels and, making my spirit into a horse, I can give someone a ride. I'll never have to be carried around again!

"Listen, when people are on the receiving end, it's because of the moment; and when they're on the losing end, it's just the order of things. If you'll be at peace with the moment and sit yourself down in the order of things, sorrow and joy will not be able to enter in. Long ago, this was called 'breaking free of your shackles.'" —*Chuang Tzu*, Chap. 24

Tzu Lai suddenly became ill. Coughing and hacking, he was about to die. His wife and children surrounded him and were in tears. Tzu Li came around to ask after him and said, "Stop all that and get back! Don't get in the way of the transformation."

Leaning against the door, he spoke with Tzu Lai. "This transformation and creativity is terrific, isn't it? What is it going to make out of you next? Where will it send you off to now? Perhaps it will make you into a rat's liver. Or how about a bug's arm?"

Tzu Lai said, "As a child is to his father and mother, he simply obeys their commands, going east, west, south, or north. As a man is to *yin* and *yang*, is it not simply the same as with father and mother? They have now brought me close to death, and if I will hear nothing of it, would that not be rather rude? What fault do they have? Listen, the Great God gives us form and troubles us with life, has us content, and rest in old age. Thus, if we consider our life good, should we not consider our death good as well?"

—*Chuang Tzu*, Chap. 6

34 *Doctrine of the Mean*, Chap. 14.

35 The Chinese character for "stink" (臭) is a compound of "self" (自) and "great" (大).

36 Picking chrysanthemums beneath the eastern hedge

Gazing leisurely at the southern mountains
The energy of the mountain is wonderful day and night
Birds flying home in pairs
Within this there is a deep and true meaning
But when I want to explain it, I have already forgotten the words.

—Tao Yuan-ming (367–427)

TAO TE CHING
CANTO I, VERSES 1–37

1 Listen, even before the beginning, the Way had no boundaries; even before the beginning, words had no consistency. —*Chuang Tzu*, Chap. 2

2 This is a standard translation, and context would indicate that it is what "Lao Tzu" may have intended. The difference in style between this and the following verse, however, suggests that the two verses had different origins and do not necessarily follow each other. Reading the characters in a slightly different way, I prefer the the following interpretation:

Everybody understands fabricated beauty to be beautiful, but it is nothing but ugliness. Everybody understands fabricated good to be good, but it is nothing but bad.

3 See the Introduction for a discussion on "fabrication."
[Such men . . .] wander free and easy, practicing nonfabrication.
—*Chuang Tzu*, Chap. 6
The Way has its reality and its telltale signs, but it does not fabricate and has no manifest form. —*Chuang Tzu*, Chap. 6

4 In a world where virtue has truly arrived, the clever are not respected, and professionals are not employed. —*Chuang Tzu*, Chap. 13

5 Dogs made of straw are used for exorcism rites at certain festivals. When the festival is over, the straw dogs are thrown away.

6 Dark and mysterious female: 玄牝, or *genbin*: This is the yin, the valley, the keyhole; the womb, the place from which all creatures enter the world.

7 Modern scholarship tends to understand these lines more along the following:
Puts himself last, but [is invited to] the fore;
Puts himself outside, but [is welcomed] within.

The text does not seem to warrant this interpretation, but it adds an interesting nuance to the meaning.

Thus, I make one big victory out of all my many little defeats. Only the sage is capable of doing such a thing. —*Chuang Tzu*, Chap. 17

8   [The sage] bestows his benefits and favors on ten thousand generations, but does not fabricate love for man. —*Chuang Tzu*, Chap. 6

9   Thus it is close to the Way. Both because of the reasons stated above this line, and because it will fit any shape into which it is poured.

10   If it is too brittle, it will be broken; if it is too sharp, it will be chipped! —*Chuang Tzu*, Chap. 33

11   Mirror of the mind: 玄覽. Scholars tend to interpret the second character as "mirror," which fits neatly with the following phrase; but it is defined actually as "the most insightful depth of the mind, from which you see all creatures just as they are."

12   Opening and closing the gate of heaven. This has been interpreted in a number of ways: a) the changes of life and death, b) the functions of the depths of the mind, and c) the gate to all mysteries, as in verse 1.

13   Listen, be bright and clear, but enter into a simplicity as coarse as white silk; be without fabrication, and return to an artlessness as plain as bark. —*Chuang Tzu*, Chap. 12

14   Yet it is the nonexistence that is the wheel's utility: 常其無有車之用. There are two traditional ways of reading this line: the one provided in this translation, as well as another that goes as follows: "It is [thus] existence and nonexistence which are the wheel's utility." The same applies to the following two couplets.

15   Set the stage: 利. Although this character now means "benefit" or "profit," it originally meant something to the effect of "plowing the fields so that grains may be planted."

16   The five colors: blue, yellow, red, white, and black; the five sounds: *kung*, *shang*, *chueh*, *wei*, and *yu* on the Chinese musical scale; the five tastes: sweet, hot (spicy), sour, salty, and bitter.

17   In this verse, we may read "pain the body" as "pain your life." Likewise, "respects his body" may be read as "respects his life"; and "loves his body" as "loves his life."

18   You stare at it fixedly, but it is without shape; you listen to it carefully, but it has no voice.   —*Chuang Tzu*, Chap. 22

    You peer at it on tiptoe, but cannot see it; you pursue it as though on the chase, but cannot get your hands on it.   —*Chuang Tzu*, Chap. 14

19   The Way has no beginning and no end; creatures have both life and death, but cannot depend on their full realization. Now empty, now full, their shape does not stop with one modality. The years cannot be held to a stop, time cannot be halted. Drying up, full of breath, filled to the brim, empty as the sky—when you think they've come to an end, their beginning is at hand.   —*Chuang Tzu*, Chap. 17

    The beginning and the end is like a circle, but there is no way to follow its path.   —*Chuang Tzu*, Chap. 27

20   That is, mixing and mingling with the vulgar world.

21   The sage pierces through the obscure and the tangled, and sees through all things as one body. He doesn't know why this is so; it is his nature. He returns to his naturally given source, behaves accordingly, and makes heaven his teacher.   —*Chuang Tzu*, Chap. 25

22   The Master said, "Listen, the Way does not back down to the great, and does not lose track of the small. Thus the Ten Thousand Things are provided for. The Way is broad indeed, and there is margin enough for all."   —*Chuang Tzu*, Chap. 13

23   Fukunaga notes that 貴 (to place value on) is an abbreviation for 遺 (to forget about or abandon). This translation will follow the text as it is, however. Think broadly and value your words. The ultimate in standing by your words is turning your back on money.   —*Chuang Tzu*, Chap. 23

24   Wisdom: 智. Most often translated as "wisdom," it is constructed of the two characters 知 (to know) and 日 (day, or days), and so includes the nuance of a *hijiri*, or a man who "knows the days," i.e., auspicious days for human activities.

25   The relationships between father and son, elder brother and younger brother, and husband and wife.

26   Ornamental conduct: 義. This is generally translated as "righteousness," but it originally meant something like "a beautiful dance," or "beautiful manners." In the *Tao Te Ching*, it often means righteousness that is self-conscious or even ostentatious. It is translated as "correct" behavior in the previous verse. Human-heartedness: 仁, is made up of two radicals, for "man" and

"two," representing how people should act with each other. Again, the *Tao Te Ching* treats this important Confucian concept as one that is too self-consciously applied, and thus becomes ornamental rather than "real." It has been translated as "conscious sympathy" in the previous verse.

27 [For this reason,] simplicity is spoken of as a state of being unmixed, and purity is spoken of as not damaging one's spirit. Being able to make his body simple and pure—this is called the True Man.
—*Chuang Tzu*, Chap. 15

28 Thus it is said, "Cut off saintliness, abandon knowledge, and you will manage the world's affairs with arms outstretched."
—*Chuang Tzu*, Chap. 11

29 I still don't know if the attractive is truly attractive, or if it's truly unattractive.
—*Chuang Tzu*, Chap. 18

Everyone knows how to criticize what they do not consider attractive, but no one knows how to criticize what is already considered good.
—*Chuang Tzu*, Chap. 10

30 Your life has a limit, but knowledge is limitless. If you chase along after the limitless by means of the limited, you'll only be on shaky ground.
—*Chuang Tzu*, Chap. 3

31 Feast: A religious festival in which cows, pigs, and sheep were sacrificed and served. Interestingly, the words translated as "great feast" originally meant a "spacious corral."

32 The man of virtue sits comfortably, but doesn't think about it; puts one foot in front of the other, but harbors no feelings about good, bad, attractive, or unattractive. Within the four seas, he calls it happiness to prepare the ground for others' profit; he makes it his own tranquility to respond to their needs. Sorrowful, he is like a suckling child that has lost his mother; blankly, he is like a traveler who has lost his way.   —*Chuang Tzu*, Chap. 12

33 Each returns to its root, but is unaware of it. Mixed up, wandering, and in the dark, none departs from it for its entire life. But if they would know what it is, they will have lost it right away.   —*Chuang Tzu*, Chap. 11

34 The very highest point of arriving at the Way is dim as dusk and silent. You cannot look at it fixedly, nor listen to it carefully.   —*Chuang Tzu*, Chap. 11

35 The quintessence of the penetration of the Way is darkly cavernous and like a moonless night. The farthest reaches of the penetration of the Way is

dim as dusk and silent ... If there is no wobbling of your own quintessence, you can live a long life. *—Chuang Tzu*, Chap. 11

36 Stamp of proof: The phrase is 其中有信. The last word, commonly translated as "faith," does not fit in this context. There are a number of other
meanings to the word, among which are "truth," "mark," "sign," and
"stamp." The meaning of this phrase lies in between those words, it seems.
So, "stamp of truth," or "mark of truth."

    This quintessence is the extreme Truth. Truth is the quintessence of sin-
cerity. *—Chuang Tzu*, Chap. 31

37 The straight tree is the first to receive the ax; the well with sweet water will
be the first to run dry. *—Chuang Tzu*, Chap. 20

38 As an inchworm will bend, and then straighten out to advance.

39 A long time ago, I asked an accomplished man about this. He said, "The
man who denigrates others to make himself look good will not get the
credit. A man who has accomplished something can tumble and fall. A
man who has made a name for himself can suffer loss."
—Chuang Tzu, Chap. 30

40 There is a play on words here. The term 伐 originally meant "to cut someone's head off with a spear or halberd," and depicted a spear and its handle.
It now means both "to strike" and "to be prideful." Hence, to be prideful
about being the strong grip of the spear, rather than the humble (長),
which originally showed an old man leaning on a staff and being supporting by it in his old age. There is a lot of imagery in the archaic characters
here that does not show up in the modern (after 200 BCE) characters.
"The staff of support" means "will [live] a long time."

41 全而帰之. The translation of this last line is tentative. A number of scholars
feel that the line was mistakenly entered into the text, and have given it
diverse interpretations.

42 The most penetrating words are those you've left out.
—Chuang Tzu, Chap. 22

43 He who does not injure things will be immune from being injured by them.
—Chuang Tzu, Chap. 22

44 Although this verse is often interpreted in the past tense, to do so seems to
miss the point. What precedes Heaven and Earth has always been there. It
is manifested by Heaven and Earth (the universe) and the Ten Thousand
Things (all things in the natural world), and the process of this manifesta-

tion is Of-Itself-So, or 自然. Thus, to say that what precedes—or really, is the foundation of—Heaven and Earth "existed," seems to imply that it, too, had a beginning. Which it did not. Some Taoists explain this by stating that what precedes Heaven and Earth is in fact *ch'i*, or 氣, which the Tao then channels into the systems and particulars of nature. But *ch'i*, like matter/energy, is neither created nor destroyed.

45 It makes itself his own foundation; itself, its very own root. Long before there was a Heaven or Earth, it existed firmly since ancient of days.
—*Chuang Tzu*, Chap. 6

46 周行而不殆. An alternative translation might be, "It goes everywhere, and is always safe [at home]."

47 There is nothing more belonging to the spirits than Heaven; nothing more fecund than the Earth; nothing greater than the king.
—*Chuang Tzu*, Chap. 13

48 聖終日行. Compare with the *I Ching*: 君子終日乾乾: The Gentleman is active without stopping the entire day.

49 Mountain stream: Also defined as a route, course, or way of reasoning.

50 If know you the male, but preserve the female, you will effect a mountain stream for all under heaven. If you know the bright, but preserve the dark, you will effect a valley route for the entire world.
—*Chuang Tzu*, Chap. 33

51 According to Fukunaga, the virtue of nonaction (無為).
Being without knowledge, you will stay close to virtue; be without desire, and you will have what is called the simplicity of unvarnished wood.
—*Chuang Tzu*, Chap. 9

52 Valley. Similar to the mountain stream in note 49, but either containing or not containing water. It may be helpful to understand that the Chinese character 谷 is composed of elements meaning "opening up an entrance."

53 Listen, breaking up the simple and making it into a utensil is the carpenter's crime. —*Chuang Tzu*, Chap. 9

54 The True Men of old: their aspects were towering, and did not wane; though they seemed insufficient, they did not accept handouts; though dignified and correct, they were not stiff; though broadminded and open, they were without flowery ornament. They were content and seemed happy, I suppose, and paid little mind to anything unless it couldn't be helped. —*Chuang Tzu*, Chap. 6

55   That is, stored and at the ready.

56   I.e., in his hand.

57   Compare with this quote from *Analects*, 1:2:3: "The Gentleman is not a utensil" (君子不器).

58   Listen, peace and a lack of vexations, tranquility and simplicity, being away from the noise of the world, and nonfabrication—these are the constants of Heaven and Earth, and the true penetration of the Way and its Virtue. Thus, kings and sages find rest in them.
                                                      —*Chuang Tzu*, Chap. 13

59   The Way is without name. Because it has no name, it fabricates nothing.
                                                      —*Chuang Tzu*, Chap. 25

60   I am said to listen with understanding. This is not because I lend an ear to others, but because I lend an ear to myself. I am said to have the clarity of the sun and moon. This is not because I observe others, it is only because I observe myself.   —*Chuang Tzu*, Chap. 8

61   "Is not forgotten": The text reads 亡, which originally meant "to be put away some place and hidden," or "to put out of sight."

62   [Moving] buoyantly, he is like an unmoored boat; empty, he wanders free and easy.   —*Chuang Tzu*, Chap. 32

63   Shackle: This means to "firmly grasp," without the negative connotations we associate with the word "shackle." In the original, the character for shackles (執) indicated a stronger nuance of grasping, perhaps with more determination.

64   Fukunaga explains 大象 as "The thing that holds or contains the Great Form, i.e., the Tao."

65   The man who is able to empty himself and wander about the world—who would be able to harm him?   —*Chuang Tzu*, Chap. 20

66   When you mingle with Gentlemen, the experience is thin, like water; when you mingle with men of little character, it is sweet, like ceremonial wine.   —*Chuang Tzu*, Chap. 20

67   If you do not fabricate things, you may use everything under heaven and there will still be more at hand.
                                                      —*Chuang Tzu*, Chap. 13

68   Heaven and Earth do not act, but there is nothing left undone.
                                                      —*Chuang Tzu*, Chap. 18

If he is unbiased, he will be at peace and not contend; if he is at peace and does not contend, he will have the clarity of the sun and moon; if he has the clarity of the sun and moon, he will be empty; if he is empty, he will not act, yet nothing will be undone.   —*Chuang Tzu*, Chap. 23

The Way is not self-possessed, and thus is without name. It is without name, and thus does not act. It does not act, but nothing is left undone.
                                                        —*Chuang Tzu*, Chap. 25

CANTO II, VERSES 38–81

69 Wang Pi (226–49), in his highly respected commentaries on the *Tao Te Ching*, noted the following:

The nature of the myriad things is spontaneity. It should be followed but not interfered with.... The sage understands Nature perfectly and knows clearly the condition of all things. Therefore, he goes along with them but takes no unnatural action. He is in harmony with them, but does not impose anything on them.   —Chan, p. 322

Thus, anything that requires conscious action or fabrication is by definition "unnatural action." It is acting by form rather than by essence. Following the Way and the Virtue of the Way must be done spontaneously or they will be "imposed" on the natural flow of things. Humanheartedness seems to occupy a midpoint between true virtue on the one hand and righteousness and etiquette on the other.

70 Truthful people act with loyalty, but are not aware of it; hitting the mark, they stand by their words, but know nothing of it.
                                                        —*Chuang Tzu*, Chap. 12

Good manners are the flower of the Way [rather than the fruit], and are the headwaters of disorder.   —*Chuang Tzu*, Chap. 22

71 Heaven obtains the One and becomes pure; Earth obtains the One and is at peace.   —*Chuang Tzu*, Chap. 18

72 The Way is the very ground of the Ten Thousand Things. When anything loses it, it dies; when something gains it, it lives.   —*Chuang Tzu*, Chap. 31

In the very beginning, there is nothing. There is nothing at hand and no names. This is when the One arises. This One is at hand, but there is still no form. Creatures obtain this and sprout with life, and this is called virtue.
                                                        —*Chuang Tzu*, Chap. 12

73 If Heaven did not receive this, it would not be high; if Earth did not receive it, it would not be broad; if the sun and moon did not receive it, they would not go on their rounds; if the Ten Thousand Things did not receive it, they would not flourish. Such is indeed the Way.

—*Chuang Tzu*, Chap. 22

Listen, the Way . . . spiritualizes the demons, and spiritualizes the king. It gives birth to Heaven, and gives birth to Earth.

—*Chuang Tzu*, Chap. 6

74 At once a dragon, at once a snake: transforming with the times.

—*Chuang Tzu*, Chap. 20

Dragon and snake share the same basic form, but one is the powerful creature that rides the winds and brings us the rain, while the other is the lowly animal that crawls along in the dirt. Nevertheless, the latter is perhaps more real flesh and blood, much as stones and their rumbling sound are more indicative of the solid and firm.

75 The kanji is simply 弱, the common word for "weak." The archaic character shows a double bow 弓, and so depicts the quality of bending. Fukunaga says that "Lao Tzu's 'weak' meant the willowy and graceful nature of a woman," and the "pliability, flexibility, and litheness of water," so "bending and flexible" seemed appropriate here, though there is some overlap today in the meanings of the two words.

76 In the very beginning, there is nothing: there is nothing at hand, and no names.   —*Chuang Tzu*, Chap. 12

77 He hears of the Way a hundred times, and still considers no one to be as good as himself.   —*Chuang Tzu*, Chap. 20

78 大器晩成 Commentators note that the "great vessel" (大器) indicates a huge bell or tripod which is "finished late," or, not easily made. The general interpretation of the phrase, however, has it that "Great genius matures late."

79 Listen, the Way is pure and stands by its word. It does not fabricate and has no shape.   —*Chuang Tzu*, Chap. 6

80 Though the sage does not live in the mountains and forests, his virtue is hidden! It is hidden, and thus he does not hide himself.

—*Chuang Tzu*, Chap. 16

81 Change attends to the [intrinsic] value of the Ten Thousand Things, but does not rely on the people.   —*Chuang Tzu*, Chap. 7

82 Scholars consider this, the 一気, variously interpreted as the *ch'i* of Heaven and Earth, the fundamental strength of the Ten Thousand Things, or the First Breath.

In the beginning, there is nothing: there is nothing at hand and no names. This is when the One arises. This One is at hand, but there is still no form. Creatures obtain this and sprout with life, and this is called virtue.

—*Chuang Tzu*, Chap. 12

83 Yin and yang.

84 The harmonized fundamental *ch'i* within Heaven and Earth.

85 The 41st hexagram of the *I Ching*: The lower decreases, but the upper increases.

86 The 42nd hexagram of the *I Ching*: The upper decreases, but the lower increases.

87 Exhort. The character is 教, the modern word for "teach." Archaically, it means "teach" as well, but with an interesting twist: fully one-half of the character depicts a whip, and the old definition is to "have someone (or something) learn by hitting him (or it) with a whip." Thus, I thought "exhort" captures the original meaning better than "teach."

88 無有: I.e., the Way.

89 Speaking thunderously, yet as silent as deep water.

—*Chuang Tzu*, Chap. 14

Thus it is said: "No Words." If you speak with No Words, you may speak to the end of your life, and have never said anything at all. Or, you may not say anything to the end of your life, and have never stopped speaking.

—*Chuang Tzu*, Chap. 27

90 Lao Tzu said, "Here is the warp and woof of preserving your life: Can you embrace the One? Can you, then, not lose it? Can you understand ill omens and bad without the cracks on turtle shells or bamboo divining sticks?" —*Chuang Tzu*, Chap. 23

91 Heaven's Way moves round and about, but does not stop to accumulate.

—*Chuang Tzu*, Chap. 13

92 Fukunaga has this as increasing knowledge and decreasing desires.

93 The person who keeps to the Way decreases daily; he decreases and then decreases again. Thus, he arrives at nonfabrication. Nothing is fabricated, yet nothing is left undone. —*Chuang Tzu*, Chap. 22

94 If you untie the knots of your mind, weed out your spirit, and are vague and soulless, the Ten Thousand Things—like rising clouds—will each return to the root. Each will return to the root, but will be unaware of it. Mixed up, wandering and in the dark, they will not depart from it for their entire lives. —*Chuang Tzu*, Chap. 11

The men of old lived in the midst of wandering and chaos; yet, remaining in such a world, they obtained a grace and lack of greed along the way. —*Chuang Tzu*, Chap. 16

95 This couplet is ambiguous at best. Those who "follow along after life" have been defined as possibly "the soft and flexible" or "the long-lived" or both. Likewise, those who "follow along after death" may be interpreted as "the hard and the strong," "the short-lived," or again, both.

96 Wild horned buffalo. Also interpreted as a species of rhinoceros.

97 死地: The place of death, the jaws of death, or a dangerous place or position.

98 Listen, the Way covers and envelopes the Ten Thousand Things. —*Chuang Tzu*, Chap. 12

99 兌: The 58th hexagram of the *I Ching*, indicating that if your spirit is correct, your affairs will go well. Here, "leaks" is interpreted as the "holes," or doors of perception: the eyes, ears, mouth, nose, etc.

100 The passions and desires that open up to the temptations and seductions of the world.

101 Vague pronouns here and elsewhere are left that way purposely rather than assigning meaning to them. The text, of course, has no object at all. "It" is somehow understood. We may assume it to be the "Tao," but Lao Tzu has left this unclear. I thought it best to do likewise. The same goes for "this" as, again, no object is in the original. To make clear where there is no clarity takes away from the Taoist emphasis on intuition and imagination. Plus, to put in something that is just flat out not there might be a little presumptuous. As with all those Zen and Taoist paintings that are mostly blank space, even the unstated has meaning.

102 To place the Way on high is the virtue of kings and princes; to give it low status is the Way of the dark and mysterious sage and the kingly man of no rank. If you apply such to yourself, retire and enjoy life leisurely, you will be followed by the recluses who live along the rivers and seas, and in the mountains and forests. Continue in this Way and soothe the world. Thus, your success will be great, your name will be Manifest, and all under Heaven will become one. —*Chuang Tzu*, Chap. 13

103 If men hold on to this virtue, then in all under Heaven there will be no warped or biased thoughts. —*Chuang Tzu*, Chap. 10

104 Truth is the utmost reach of pure sincerity. —*Chuang Tzu*, Chap. 31

105 I maintain the One, and sit down, legs outstretched, in harmony.
—*Chuang Tzu*, Chap. 11

106 The man who has arrived makes harmony his measure, and floats along free and easy with the ancestor of the Ten Thousand Things.
—*Chuang Tzu*, Chap. 20

107 I always depend on the Of-Itself-So, and do not try to add to life.
—*Chuang Tzu*, Chap. 5

108 See note 42.

109 See note 100.

110 Fukunaga defines this as "Forgetting words and knowledge, and becoming one with the Way." Elsewhere, it is interpreted as hiding one's talents and knowledge, and becoming a companion of the common folk. Also, being equal and without distinctions.

111 I am at the point of taking an aimless walk to look about in the four directions. How could I arrive at the leisure where one considers some men valuable and others worthless? —*Chuang Tzu*, Chap. 21

112 Ahh, this is nurturing the mind. You only reside in nonfabrication, and creatures transform of themselves. —*Chuang Tzu*, Chap. 11

113 The men of old who nurtured the world had no desires and all under heaven was sufficient; they acted without fabrication and the Ten Thousand Things were transformed; they were as peaceful as a deep pool and the people were settled. . . . Act with No Mind, and the gods and demons will follow along after you. —*Chuang Tzu*, Chap. 12

114 The above four lines are contrary to modern scholarly interpretation, yet seem to follow the text, both in etymological terms and in the flow of meaning.

115 Life and death, beginning and end, act just like day and night, and this is not to confuse you. And the same hardly needs to be said about gain and loss, or good fortune or bad. People will toss off their underlings just as they would mud or dirt. They understand that their own lives are more valued than having underlings. What is valued exists in yourself and is not lost in the changes around you. All the more so with the ten thousand changes that from the very beginning have no limits.
—*Chuang Tzu*, Chap. 21

116 The Ten Thousand Things are One. That which is beautiful is considered to be something wonderful. That which is ugly is considered like the smell of something rotting. But the smell of something rotting again changes and creates something wonderful. Something wonderful again changes to the smell of something rotting. Thus it is said: "All under heaven is pierced with one single *ch'i*." Therefore the sage values the One.

—*Chuang Tzu*, Chap. 22

117 If the fate of the times is not appropriate and you are in difficult straits in the world, make your roots deep, be at ease with the ridgepole of things, and wait. This is the Way of keeping yourself in one place.

—*Chuang Tzu*, Chap. 16

118 When cooking a small fish, the less you do, the better. Spices, breadcrumbs, and fancy oils will only spoil the taste. Simply put it in the frying pan and cook.

119 Therefore, if the Gentleman, unavoidably, must go out and confront the world, there is nothing better than nonfabrication.

—*Chuang Tzu*, Chap. 11

Thus, it is said: If he moves, it is like Heaven; if he is at peace and does not contend, he is like the Earth. Settled with his mind One, he is the king of all under Heaven. He will not be punished by demons, and his spirit will not tire. Settled with his mind One, the Ten Thousand Things will follow along behind. —*Chuang Tzu*, Chap. 13

120 This would not have been a kitchen as we have them now, but was the place where the large earthenware ovens were kept and operated.

121 See verse 27: Therefore the sage always saves men from their mistakes in a goodly fashion, and thus no one is thrown overboard.

122 The Three Ministers: The Grand Tutor, the Assistant Grand Tutor, and the Grand Protector. These officials were appointed from among the high nobles, and, as the closest advisers to the emperor, their positions and authority were directly beneath his.

123 Lao Tzu said, "Quite so.... If the Way could be proposed to a superior, there should be no one who would not propose it to his parents."

—*Chuang Tzu*, Chap. 14

124 At the time of this writing, one *li* equaled about 360 paces. It is now standardized at 500 meters, or about 550 yards.

125 If something is acted upon, there is going to be damage.

—*Chuang Tzu*, Chap. 20

126 The man who has arrived concocts nothing; the great sage makes nothing up.   —*Chuang Tzu*, Chap. 22

Only nonfabrication is close to being alive.   —*Chuang Tzu*, Chap. 18

127 Return (反). There are a number of characters in the Chinese lexicon meaning "return." This character represents a hand turning over, and thus implies repetition of an action or process. But it has also come to mean "returning to the foundation." It is also often synonymous with another return: 復, which is the important 24th hexagram of the *I Ching*, indicating the eternal cycle and restoration of all things.

128 Sweep your own individual nature clean, and you will return to Virtue. If you penetrate Virtue, it is the same as being at the Beginning. If you are the same as being at the Beginning, you will be empty. Being empty, you will be great and will accompany the straightforward and No Mind twittering of the birds. If you join in with the twittering of the birds, you may unite with the doings of Heaven and Earth. That uniting is confused and indistinct, like being stupid or dim. This is called the dark and mysterious Virtue. It is the same as the great order of things.

—*Chuang Tzu*, Chap. 12

129 Chien Wu was questioning Lien Shu, and said, "When I was listening to Chieh Yu's words, they were big, but did not hit the mark; they ran all around, but did not return."   —*Chuang Tzu*, Chap. 1

130 The warrior: 士. This is the educated warrior, a man with a solid foundation like a nail driven into the ground.

131 Return to the essentials, and speak of the farthest reaches of things.

—*Chuang Tzu*, Chap. 17

132 No-Beginning said, "Not to know is deep! To know is shallow! Not to know is the pith! To know is the shell!" At this point, Great Purity looked up to the heavens, sighed, and said, "Not to know is to know? To know is not to know? Who can know this knowing that does not know?" No-Beginning said, "The Way cannot be heard; if it *is* heard, it is not the Way. The Way cannot be seen; if it is seen, it is not the Way. The Way cannot be definitively spoken of; if it is, it is not the Way. Did you know that it's the shapeless that shapes the shaped? The Way cannot be given a name that hits the mark."   —*Chuang Tzu*, Chap. 22

133 Or, "Just consider sickness to be sickness."

134 He who is sick can speak well of his own sickness. He who is sick of sickness is no longer sick. (Or, "He who considers sickness to be sickness is not sick.") —*Chuang Tzu*, Chap. 23

135 Or, likewise, "Because he considers sickness to be sickness . . . "

136 Heaven's net is the net heaven throws out to catch evil people. It is a natural working of the Of-Itself-So. This sounds more like the Buddhist idea of karma, but it is straight from the old man's mouth. In the story that follows, Chuang Tzu is playing with Lao Tzu's phrase, "though wide-meshed, nothing slips through." The butcher points out that any aperture is wide enough for his knife, as he works with the Tao of things. Heaven's net can be wide-meshed and nothing that acts contrary to the Tao will slip through, but the narrow space between the joints will let the blade slip through altogether because he acts in accordance with nature.

In Chapter 3 of the *Chuang Tzu*, a butcher speaks to the ruler, discussing why his knife is still sharp after using it for many years, even though he has never put it to the whetstone: "The knife blade is not thick. Because of this lack of thickness, wherever there is an aperture, it enters in, and that aperture seems broad and wide. In applying the blade, then, there will invariably be plenty of margin."

137 Official executioner: the same as heaven's net.

138 A number of scholars think that the Chinese character here 共, "to be used as furnishing for the wealthy," is a mistake in the text, and should be 折, "to break."

The straight tree will be the first to receive the ax. The well with sweet water will be the first to be used up. —*Chuang Tzu*, Chap. 20

139 The filial child obtains medicine and, with a thin and wasted expression [from having expended all his time and effort], prepares it for his loving father. The sage would find this embarrassing. —*Chuang Tzu*, Chap. 12

140 During the Chou dynasty, a promissory note for a bill was written on a strip of wood and split into two. The left half was for the creditor, the right half for the debtor.

141 Knotting cords: In high antiquity, in the days before writing, cords were knotted to record events, agreements in bartering, and the affairs of state.

142 Great oratory does not speak out loud. —*Chuang Tzu*, Chap. 2

In discussing this matter, you will not necessarily come to a great understanding.   —*Chuang Tzu*, Chap. 22

Note: Quibble, oratory, and discussion are all possible translations of the
Chinese character 弁, the first character in the word 弁護士, lawyer.

143 You may become a know-it-all in this matter, but not necessarily know
anything.   —*Chuang Tzu*, Chap. 22

144 The sage moves about on the Way, but hoards (or, accumulates) nothing.
                                                  —*Chuang Tzu*, Chap. 13

By his hoarding, he creates lack.   —*Chuang Tzu*, Chap. 33

TAOISM AND ZEN

1   Welch, *Taoism: The Parting of the Way*, p. 119.

2   Ibid., p. 125

3   For other fascinating developments in Taoism, see Welch's *Taoism: The
Parting of the Way*.

4   Other guesses at this date include 516, 470, and 527.

5   For those interested, the Chinese characters for Hsiung-erh Feng are 熊耳峯.

6   Bodhidharma, however, did seem to have his favorite text, the
Lankavatara Sutra. This work teaches, in part, the avoidance of dualism,
and begins—uncharacteristically for Buddhist sutras, but not so strange
for Zen—with the Buddha himself having a great belly laugh.

7   Their shapes and *ch'i* are different, but in nature they are equal.
    None can take the place of the other, but their lives are all replete, and
their allotments are all sufficient. How can I know what is vast and what
minute? How can I know what is long and what short? How can I know
what is the same, what different?   —*Lieh Tzu*

8   Pu Tai (Japanese: Hotei), the tenth-century Korean monk who has been
deified as the fat laughing Buddha carrying a large bag of blessings, modified
this "following circumstances" (随緣) to "following the moment" (随時).

9   Confucius was sightseeing in Lu-liang. There was a place where the water
plummeted thirty fathoms, then bubbled and flowed and splashed along
for another forty *li*, so that neither fishes nor water creatures could swim

there. He noticed a man swimming in just that spot, and so thought the man was suffering some pain and wanted to die. He ordered his disciples to line up along the current to rescue the man. But after a few hundred paces, the man got out on his own and walked leisurely along the embankment, letting his hair fall where it might, and singing a song as he went. Confucius followed along after him and asked, "I took you for a demon, now I realize you are a man. I would like to ask if you have some Way of treading the water." The man said, "No, I have no Way at all. I start with my beginnings, grow with my character, and complete things with my destiny. I enter along with the whirlpools, and come out where it's calm; I follow the Way of the water, and do not consider myself. For this reason, I'm able to tread along." Confucius said, "What do you mean when you say, 'I start with my beginnings, grow with my character, and complete things with my destiny'?" The man said, "I was born on land and felt repose on the land. This was my beginning. I grew up in the water and felt repose in the water. This is my character. Not knowing why, I naturally do what I do. This is my destiny." —*Chuang Tzu*, Chap. 19

10 My friend Prof. Richard Carter appended this to: Zen is Indian Buddhism with Chinese jokes.

11 The wild buffalo finds no place to thrust its horns,
The tiger finds no place to sink its claws.   —VERSE 50

12 The classic example of this comes from the twenty-first case of the *Wumen Kuan*, the collection of koans published in 1229. When the master Yunmen is asked, "What is the Buddha?" his reply is "A dried dung stick."

13 In the *Chieh Tzu Yuan Hua Chuan*, or *The Mustard Seed Garden Manual of Painting* (Sze, p. 129), we find this typical comment:
    In estimating people, their quality of spirit (*ch'i* 氣) is as basic as the way they are formed: and so it is with the rocks, which are also the framework of the Heavens and Earth and also have *ch'i*. . . .To depict rocks with *ch'i*, it must be sought beyond the material and in the intangible.

14 With all their comings and goings, human activities are almost infinite.
    Who can know what is evil, what is good?
    Good and evil are at best mutually shaped.
    You praise or blame whichever way the wind blows.   —Tao Yuan-ming

15 There is a single element that runs through my Tao.   —*Lun Yu*, 4:15

1   Duke Ling of Wei asked Confucius [Chung-ni] about military affairs. Confucius replied, "Up to this time I have listened to matters related to sacrificial dishes, but have not yet taken up the study of troops in the field," and left the premises.   —*Analects*, 15:1

2   The Master said, "Meng Chih-fan was not proud [of his courage]. When his troops were in retreat, he brought up the rear. As he was entering the fortress gates, he whipped his horse and said, It's not that I dared to take up the rear guard, but my horse wouldn't go fast.'   —*Analects*, 6:15

3   See Introduction, note 3.

4   *The Classic of Changes: A New Translation of the I Ching as Interpreted by Wang Bi*, p. 26.

5   Virtue (德): The strength and integrity of your own inborn talents and character. See the discussion of this term in the Introduction.

6   "Easy" and "change" are the same character (易) in Chinese.

7   The term "Tao" was not the exclusive property of the "Taoists." Chung-ni referred to it often, and Sun Tzu declared that the very first factor to be considered in the art of war is the Tao. In Chapter IV, 16, he goes on to say that "The best strategist cultivates the Tao."

8   Other Taoist books eventually crossed over the straits from Korea as well, but by this time, "Taoism" had been thoroughly mixed with Chinese folk religion, medicine, and general lore. Japan was fertile ground for such material, which soon became part and parcel of the indigenous folk and mountain religions, even making its appearance in the special gods of the household. With assimilation, however, origins often become clouded, and the ancient significance of words, concepts, and even familiar objects may be lost. Even today, one may find moss-covered stone statues of strong Taoist influence on the edge of mountain villages, the meaning of which have long been forgotten by the local population. When hiking along the Kiso Kaido, an ancient road running through central Japan, this translator found a number of such statues along the way. When asked about their significance, even the older villagers usually responded with something like, "*Saa, washira shiran kedo na.*" "Well, we really have no idea, you know." So, too, with words and philosophies.

9   Mt. Kurama is an area famously inhabited by *tengu*, a sort of goblin of Chinese origins, famous for their ability at swordsmanship and well-versed in Taoist and Zen philosophies. The priests mentioned above may indeed have been the *tengu* who later taught the martial arts to young Minamoto Yoshitsune.

10   See note 8 to Taoism and Zen.

11   Look, *ch'i* controls form by riding the mind. In this way, the function of the body is entirely grasped by *ch'i*. Now, *ch'i*'s spirit is called the mind, and when the mind is equipped with the principles of heaven, it makes *ch'i* its foundation. The essence of the mind originally has no shape, sound, color, or smell; but when it rides *ch'i*, it performs these functions. *Ch'i* pervades above and below. If you have but the smallest thought, it is possessed by *ch'i*. It moves when in contact with things in the mind. This is called emotion. When thinking, it goes back and forth, conceptualizing. But when the mind and perceptions move just as they are and your true character is in accord with the principles of heaven, the spirit is pierced through from beginning to end. The *ch'i* does not move without reason.

    This is like a boat following a current downstream. Though you can say that it moves, the boat is at rest and there is no trace of that movement. This is called "moving without moving."

—*The Demon's Sermon on the Martial Arts,* Chap. 1

BIBLIOGRAPHY

WORKS IN ORIENTAL LANGUAGES

Chang Chung-yuan. *Roshi no Shiso*. Translated into Japanese by Ueno Hiromichi. Tokyo: Kodansha Gakujitsu Bunko, 1987.

Chang Wan-shou, ed. *Hsin I Lieh Tzu Tushu*. Taipei: Sanmin Shushu, 1994.

Fukunaga Mitsuji and Kozen Hiroshi. *Roshi-Soshi*. Tokyo: Chikuma Shobo, 2004.

Iriya Yoshitaka, ed. *Kanzan*. Tokyo: Iwanami Shoten, 1958.

Itsukai Tomoyoshi, ed. *Toen-mei*. Tokyo: Iwanami Shoten, 1958.

Kaizuka Shigeki et al., eds. *Kadokawa Kanwa Chujiten*. Tokyo: Kadokawa Shoten, 1960, 1976.

Kanaya Osamu, ed. *Rongo*. Tokyo: Iwanami Shoten, 1963.

———, ed. *Roshi*. Tokyo: Kodansha Gakujutsu Bunkyo, 1997.

Kusuyama Haruki. *Roshi Nyumon*. Tokyo: Kodansha Gakujutsu Bunko, 2002.

Morohashi Tetsuji. *Daikanwa Jiten*. 16 vols. Tokyo: Daishukan Shoten, 1956.

Nakamura Hajime and Kino Kazuyoshi, eds. *Hannya Shingyo / Kongo Hannyakyo*. Tokyo: Iwanami Shoten, 1960.

Nihon Daijiten Kankokai, ed. *Nihon Kokugo Daijiten*. 20 vols. Tokyo: Shogakkan, 1977.

Nishida Kitaro. *Zen no Kenkyu*. Tokyo: Iwanami Shoten, 1950.

———. *Tetsugaku no Konpon Mondai*. 2 vols. Tokyo: Iwanami Shoten, 2005.

Nomura Shigeo. *Roshi-Soshi*. Tokyo: Kadokawa Bunko, 2004.

Ogawa Tamaki. *Roshi*. Tokyo: Chuokoron-shinsha, 1973.

Okudaira Takashi and Omura Masao. *Roshi-Resshi*. Tokyo: Tokuma Shoten, 2004.

Osaki Yujiro, ed. *Setsubun Kaiji (The Annotated Shuo Wen)*. Tokyo: Tokai Daigaku Shuppankai, 1991.

Shibayama Zenkei. *Zenrin Kushu*. Kyoto: Kichudo, 1985.

Shimada Kenji, ed. *Daigaku-chuyo*. Tokyo: Asahi Shimbunsha, 1967.

Shirakawa Shizuka. *Jito*. Tokyo: Heibonsha, 1985.

Takada Shinji and Goto Motomi, eds. and trans. *Ekkyo*, vol. 1. Tokyo: Iwanami Bunsho, 2004.

Takeuchi Yoshio. *Roshi no Kenkyu*. Tokyo: Kaizosha, 1927.

Todo Myoho, ed. *Gakken Kanwa Daijiten*. Tokyo: Gakushu kenkyusha, 1989.

Yoshikawa Kojiro, ed. *Toen-mei*. Tokyo: Iwanami Shoten, 1958.

WORKS IN ORIENTAL LANGUAGES AND ENGLISH

Blyth, R. H. *Oriental Humor*. Tokyo: The Hokuseido Press, 1959.

———. *Zen and Zen Classics, Vol. 1*. Tokyo: The Hokuseido Press, 1960.

———. *Zen and Zen Classics, Vol. 4: Mumonkan*. Tokyo: The Hokuseido Press, 1966.

WORKS IN ENGLISH

Callicot, J. Baird, and Roger T. Ames, eds. *Nature in Asian Traditions of Thought*. Albany: State University of New York Press, 1989.

Chan, Wing-tsit. *A Sourcebook in Chinese Philosophy*. Princeton: Princeton University Press, 1963.

Eberhard, Wolfram. *A History of China*. Berkeley: University of California Press, 1977.

Eliade, Mircea. *Shamanism: Archaic Techniques of Ecstasy*. Princeton: Princeton University Press, 1964.

Eliot, T. S. *Four Quartets*. London: Harcourt, Inc., 1943.

Fairbank, John, Edwin Reischauer, and Albert Craig. *East Asia: Tradition and Transformation*. Boston: Houghton Mifflin Company, 1978.

Hawkes, David. *Ch'u Tz'u: The Songs of the South*. London: Oxford University Press, 1959.

Issai Chozanshi. Trans. William Scott Wilson. *The Demon's Sermon on the Martial Arts*. Boston: Shambhala Publications, 2012.

Keizan Zenji. *The Denkoroku*. Mount Shasta, CA: Shasta Abbey, 1993.

Liu, James T. C., and Wei-ming Tu, eds. *Traditional China*. Englewood Cliffs: Prentice Hall, Inc., 1970.

Lynn, Richard John. *The Classic of Changes: A New Translation of the I Ching as Interpreted by Wang Bi*. New York: Columbia University Press, 2004.

Morris, Ivan, ed. *Madly Sing in the Mountains*. New York: Walker & Company, 1970.

Red Pine, trans. *Lao Tzu's Tao Te Ching*. San Francisco: Mercury House, 1996.

Shen, C. Y. Fu, et al. *Traces of the Brush: Studies in Chinese Calligraphy*. New Haven: Yale University Press, 1977.

Suzuki, D. T., trans. *The Lankavatara Sutra*. Taipei: SMC Publishing Inc., 1991.

Sze, Mai-mai, ed. and trans. *The Mustard Seed Garden Manual of Painting*. Princeton: Princeton University Press, 1956.

Waley, Arthur. *The Nine Songs: A Study of Shamanism in China*. London: George Allen & Unwin, 1955.

Wang, Fang-yu. *Introduction to Chinese Cursive Script*. New Haven: Far Eastern Publications, 1958.

Watson, Burton. *Early Chinese Literature*. New York: Columbia University Press, 1962.

Welch, Holmes. *Taoism: The Parting of the Way*. Boston: Beacon Press, 1971

BOOKS AND TRANSLATIONS
BY WILLIAM SCOTT WILSON

The Book of Five Rings, by Miyamoto Musashi

Cultivating Ch'i: A Samurai Physician's Teachings on the Way of Health,
by Kaibara Ekiken

The Demon's Sermon on the Martial Arts: And Other Tales, by Issai Chozanshi

Hagakure: The Book of the Samurai, by Yamamoto Tsunetomo

The Life-Giving Sword: Secret Teachings from the House of the Shogun,
by Yagyu Munenori

The Lone Samurai: The Life of Miyamoto Musashi

Master of the Three Ways: Reflections of a Chinese Sage on Living a Satisfying Life,
by Hung Ying-ming

The One Taste of Truth: Zen and the Art of Drinking Tea

Tao Te Ching: A New Translation, by Lao Tzu

The Unfettered Mind: Writings from a Zen Master to a Master Swordsman,
by Takuan Sōhō